"For those who question if God cares what they are going through, Abby McDonald's wise and thoughtful insights provide a perspective shift to discouraged hearts. Learn to hang on to hope through difficult circumstances as you see God's trustworthy nature displayed with each turn of the page."

—**Katie M. Reid,** author of *Made Like Martha: Good News for the Woman Who Gets Things Done*

"Abby comes alongside her reader like a safe friend, inviting you to step out of the fog and see the road in front of you with new eyes. Her vulnerable stories reminded me God has not forgotten my heartache, and he is whispering grace over me even when my spiritual sight is limited. *Shift* will help you change your perspective and move forward through the hard seasons of life with renewed hope."

—**Lyli Dunbar,** speaker, life coach, and writer for the Proverbs 31 Ministries First 5 App and at Love God Greatly

"Fresh and loving insight that goes straight to the heart. Abby will stun you with her inspiring words anchored in biblical truth. A lighthouse of hope!"

—**Jami Amerine,** author of *Stolen Jesus* and *Sacred Ground, Sticky Floors*

"Abby McDonald's heart for her readers is evident in her every word. Genuine and gentle, she leads us to a place where we can shift our lenses to see God's presence in *all* moments—good, bad, and in between. Because, as much as we like to focus on the highs and lows, God longs to meet us in the middle. Abby's practical approach in *Shift* will help you see him there."

—**Kelly O'Dell Stanley,** author of *Praying Upside Down, Designed to Pray,* and *InstaPrayer*

"As new believers or seasoned Christ-followers, we all have times when we struggle to maintain the right perspective. In *Shift*, Abby McDonald opens our eyes to the freedom we can have through a change in focus. Abby communicates as if she were sitting right here in my living room, and I can feel her genuine desire to help others grow in Christ. I can't wait to introduce her message to our women's ministry!"

—**Kristine Brown,** author of *Over It. Conquering Comparison to Live Out God's Plan* and *Over It. Devotional for Teen Girls*

"In a world that is constantly vying for our attention, it can be hard to focus on the one thing that most matters: God. *Shift* artfully met my heart with relatable stories, insightful Scripture, and fresh perspectives, many beckoning me to come closer to Jesus. As I turned page after page, there were various times that I had to stop and laugh, consider and ponder, or underline and write notes in the margin. I really enjoyed Abby's heartfelt message and storytelling."

—**Kelly Balarie,** speaker, blogger at Purposeful Faith, and author of *Fear Fighting* and *Battle Ready*

"Perspective is everything. As *Shift* illustrates, changing our focus is a gift that can empower a radical faith. Beneath her quiet, graceful demeanor, McDonald emerges here as a dynamic writer with a powerful message about the necessity of seeking God's presence in every season and situation of our lives. Inspiring readers with her own life stories along with practical, biblical principles, McDonald encourages that no matter the struggle, you can discover a deeper wisdom and a stronger faith in the process that will transform your life. Sometimes all it takes is one small *shift.*"

—**Lisa Murray,** licensed marriage and family therapist and author of *Peace for a Lifetime: Embracing a Life of Hope, Wholeness, and Harmony through Emotional Abundance*

shift

shift

Changing Our Focus *to* See
the Presence *of* God

Abby McDonald

LEAFWOOD
PUBLISHERS
an imprint of Abilene Christian University Press

SHIFT

Changing Our Focus to See the Presence of God

LEAFWOOD
P U B L I S H E R S
an imprint of Abilene Christian University Press

Copyright © 2020 by Abby McDonald

ISBN 978-1-68426-310-3 | LCCN 2019039875

Printed in the United States of America

Published in association with The Blythe Daniel Agency, Inc., PO Box 64197, Colorado Springs, CO 80962.

LIBRARY OF CONGRESS CATALOGING-IN-PUBLICATION DATA

Names: McDonald, Abby, author.
Title: Shift : changing our focus to see the presence of God / Abby McDonald.
Description: Abilene, Texas : Leafwood Publishers, an imprint of Abilene Christian
    University Press, 2020. | Includes bibliographical references.
Identifiers: LCCN 2019039875 | ISBN 9781684263103 (paperback)
Subjects: LCSH: Presence of God. | God—Knowableness. | God (Christianity)—Omnipresence.
Classification: LCC BT180.P6 M33 2020 | DDC 231.7—dc23
LC record available at https://lccn.loc.gov/2019039875

Cover design by ThinkPen Design | Interior text design by Sandy Armstrong, Strong Design

Leafwood Publishers is an imprint of Abilene Christian University Press
ACU Box 29138, Abilene, Texas 79699

1-877-816-4455 | www.leafwoodpublishers.com

20 21 22 23 24 25 / 7 6 5 4 3 2 1

To Chris,

My love and my biggest fan.

I love doing this wild adventure of faith with you.

Contents

Introduction

I had no idea what a 4D movie was, but I was about to find out. It was the middle of Christmas break, and my parents had just bought our little family tickets to *The Polar Express*. In 4D.

Everything appeared to be like a normal 3D movie. The attendant handed us glasses to view the show. We entered a theater that looked similar to most other movie theaters I'd been to. Then, the show started, and my seat jolted. It felt like I was actually on a train. When the waiters danced through the air with hot chocolate, I could smell it. Ice blasted in my face when the train skidded across the frozen lake.

The whole experience was unlike any movie I'd ever been to, but all my youngest son saw was a blur of shapes in front of him. His strong-willed, three-year-old self refused to put on the glasses. So, while he could feel and smell the sensations of the adventure, he couldn't see it. Not clearly, anyway. He completely missed the visual part of the show.

Do you ever feel as though you're missing God? Perhaps you had a strong sense of his presence at the beginning of your relationship, but you hit a wall. Or maybe you're picking up the pieces of a deferred dream, wondering if you heard God wrong when you chased after it. Maybe you're in the thick of a personal or a family crisis, and you don't know how God could be in it. I think no matter how long we've been following Jesus, we eventually reach a place where we wonder, "Where is he? Did I miss him? Was that really him at all?"

These questions are what set me on the journey we're about to embark upon. There have been long, dark seasons of my life when I reached for God, but my hands came up empty. I fought against the silence and I cried out to him, wondering why he'd abandoned me. I didn't understand how I could do all the things the characteristic Christian girl would do, but still be wandering through a wilderness.

As I searched the Scriptures, prayed continually, and thought about you, dear reader, I became convinced that we don't have to wait until we're on the other side of the struggle, the wilderness, or the tired monotony of our days to know God. We can know him right here, right now. In the middle of the trouble and the confusion. But how?

What if we altered our perspective? What if, like my son who refused to wear the glasses, we're using the wrong set of tools? There's a shift that has to take place. We have to change not only how we view him, but how we look for him.

This adventure is the adventure I invite you to take with me. We will study the Psalms of David, who repeatedly felt deserted by God, and look at the shift that takes place it his heart. We will look at the first disciples and consider what made them follow a person who hadn't yet shown his power. Then, we will look at Jesus himself and examine the unique relationship he had with the Father. A relationship that fueled his mission, his purpose, and his effectiveness here on earth.

When we finish, we won't be the same. My prayer is that we'll see God with a new set of eyes and a new gait of fresh confidence. And what's even better? Others will see him too. They'll see him as we share our vision and be inspired to look for him even in the shadows. This is what newfound faith can do. Will you join me?

1

Invisible or Not?

My husband has an uncanny ability to notice people others don't. Whether it's the person with car trouble on the side of the road or a neighbor no one else seems to care about, Chris sees. He extends a helping hand when it's needed. Sometimes, this involves me and means putting my own schedule aside. *Sigh*. This happened a few months ago when my plan was to have a quiet evening at home after a crazy, chaotic week of school activities.

I'll be honest. I didn't want to have our neighbor over for dinner. It was the middle of the week in mid-September, and I was tired. The kids were still adjusting to their new classes, and I was adjusting to all that comes with a new school year. The middle-aged man who lived next door was single, quirky, and difficult to make conversation with. But he was also grieving after recently losing his dad, and my husband offered a hand of friendship. So I agreed. A roast simmered in the slow cooker.

About thirty minutes before dinnertime, I realized we were running low on drinks, so I made a quick trip to the store. I raced through the aisles, trying to make sure I got home before the timer beeped. As I was coming back up the steps into the house, I swung the door open and my heart nearly stopped as I heard a loud, "Hey, hey, hey!"

My neighbor was sitting on his walker, right beside the door. *Grace, Abby. Grace. Put on your grace face*, I kept telling myself on repeat.

He labored up to his feet, and I helped him get inside before finishing dinner prep while he made himself at home.

Later, as we sat around the table eating, we all made casual conversation and my kids were their usual, amicable selves. They wanted to tell Don about their toys, their video games, and the instruments they played. I could tell he wasn't particularly interested, but he nodded and was patient as they recalled each detail about their favorites. There was something else about him, though. Something in his face that made my heart sink.

It was his eyes. His eyes were completely void of any light or joy. I could feel his loneliness and despair as though they were shadows hanging over me. I chided myself for even questioning the idea to have him over for dinner. And silently, I prayed for him.

I prayed God would transform the heart of this man who turned his back on God and the church years ago. I prayed God would use my family to soften those layers of scar tissue, and for the Spirit to move in an undeniable way.

Two weeks later, he accepted an invitation to go to Bible study with my husband. This was his first "yes" after years of my husband asking. My heart rejoiced. I could see an immediate answer to prayer, and I praised God for the work he was doing. My husband saw it too, and described the way Don was opening up in their small men's group. We sensed a door opening, and anticipated the change that would take place in Don's life.

Then there was a shift. We didn't see him sitting in his favorite spot on the porch one afternoon. This was unusual, because he made a habit of calling out to us from his chair each afternoon. But we assumed he was napping or watching TV, and we went on with our evening.

It turns out he wasn't. He wasn't inside or even down the street at the neighborhood market. He was at the hospital. The next day, my husband received a text from his caretaker. He was in the ICU with a brain bleed. The slow, building pressure on his brain started after a fall that happened weeks earlier, but he had never gone to a doctor.

Within two weeks, he was gone. Even though the doctors expected him to make a full recovery. Even though he was responsive and alert when Chris visited him. My husband and I bowed our heads at the same dinner table where he sat weeks earlier, unable to comprehend the news of his passing.

Did we misunderstand what God was doing? Were my husband's efforts to reach out to this man in vain? We don't have the answers. We don't know if Don called on the name of the Lord in his final hours, or if his spirit is at rest.

The suddenness of the experience jarred us and left us walking in darkness for days. The circle of people who cared about him was so small, we had no one to look to for answers. We had no one to ask about his demeanor before the slip. We had no contact to ask if his eyes lit with hope during the hours spent in the hospital. When FedEx would deliver mail or neighbors would ask about the lights that stayed on at his house, we felt at a complete loss. Did anyone know him? Did anyone care?

Experiences like this one can leave us reeling, searching for answers. We catch a glimpse of something God is doing in the heavenly realms, but then things don't turn out the way we think they should. We sense God moving and working in someone's life, but then a door slams shut before we have the chance to see real change.

These moments have the ability to crush our faith. We wonder where God is and why he isn't responding to the cries of our hearts. We want others to see his power and his ability to change a life, but he seems distant. Unresponsive.

How do we keep our eyes locked on the Author and Finisher of our faith even when our faith is faltering? How do we keep our focus fixed on the Savior even when the person we prayed for isn't saved? We need to shift our perspective. We need to look at the work he's already doing instead of the answer we haven't received. God was, in fact, working. Others saw it. My husband and I just didn't see it at the time.

If you've ever walked with God through difficult seasons, you've likely asked some of these same questions. Questions don't mean absence of faith, but show we are growing in our faith. We're seeing how God makes his presence known in our lives.

One of the beautiful things about God is that he can handle our questions and doubts. He doesn't turn away from our uncertainty, but invites us to know him more. He invites us to look beyond what we can see and get to know who he is as a Father, a person, and a friend. Even when we don't understand what he's doing, we can know his heart as he knows ours. He honors the way we earnestly seek him in the midst of our doubt and grief.

Trusting the Guide

When I was a little girl, our family traveled to the Blue Ridge Mountains every summer. One of our favorite hiking spots was

Mt. Pisgah, which is distinguished by a huge television broadcast tower at the peak. At the base of the mountain, the view of this metal and wire steeple is unobstructed. It was our beacon at the top—our goal. There was no questioning when we arrived at our final destination, because the summit had a clear marker.

However, once we started along the trail, the view of the tower was obscured. Trees towered all around us. We could see the trail in front of us, but our destination was only discernable at various clearings on our way to the top. We had to trust that those who mapped the trail knew what they were doing. We paid attention to signs telling us which way to go. We knew our stopping place was still there, but our faith was not in what we could see. Our faith came from what we saw when we had a clear, unobstructed view, but the obstacles didn't keep us from pressing ahead. They simply made the hike more challenging.

Often in life, our faith is like the trek up that mountain. We know Jesus and commit our lives to following him. Sometimes the life-altering experience of salvation is so transformative, we feel as though we could reach out our hand and touch him. During those first few months and maybe years of walking in the Light, we can't wait to see what he'll do next. God is real. We know it because we have tasted and seen that he is good. If he could move us and transform us in such a tangible way, how could he not be? His work in our hearts is all the evidence we need. But over time, do we have a shift in how we view our faith?

Eventually we encounter a rough season or two or more. Our prayers for a loved one aren't answered. A financial crisis hits out of nowhere, and we wonder how we're going to make it to the next paycheck. Family suffers from illness, and the pain we watch them endure sends our faith spiraling. Where is God? Is he still there even when we don't see the outcome we desire?

During these times, it is crucial that we trust our Guide. But how? How can we raise our sights up and see him like the tower on the peak when our view is obscured by life's difficulties? Like the hike up the mountain trail, we must rely on the visual markers he gives us. Even when the trail gets rocky and we can't see the summit, we must remember what compelled us to follow him in the first place. Was it his love? His grace? The lack of an answer to our prayers does not mean those attributes have changed. We must have faith that he knows the way even when we don't see where we're headed. We must trust that our Savior sees us even when we can't see the outcome. A faith that only propels us forward when we receive a clear answer will not keep us in motion for long. We need faith in the unknown. Faith in the unseen. Faith when the fog is heavy and obscures any view of the summit.

What if the struggle isn't a signal to quit, but a sign to keep going? What if the seasons when we wonder where he is are the times when he is doing some of his mightiest work?

We may not be able to see what he's doing or receive the answer to our prayer, but when we shift our view and stick close to him, others see him. They see him in our walk. They see him in our commitment to pursuing him even when the way isn't clear. As we pray and follow his commands, his Spirit is evident in our lives. Often, we're not even aware of the way his light is shining in the midst of our difficulties.

The Work We Don't See

In the last few chapters of the Gospel of John, Jesus spends much time preparing his disciples for what's to come. He teaches them, eats with them, and prays for them. He walks with them and displays the ultimate act of humility and the heart of a servant in washing their feet.

Jesus knew what was to come. He knew his closest friends would be grieving and asking questions they'd be unable to answer. In one night, he was betrayed by one of own his followers, denied by the person (Peter) who said he'd die for him, and sentenced to be killed by those who had witnessed his miracles. Murdered for a crime he never committed.

I find it no mistake that one of the last teachings Jesus gave to his disciples was about the vine and the branches. In some of his opening sentences, Jesus says, "Abide in me, and I in you. As the branch cannot bear fruit by itself, unless it abides in the vine, neither can you, unless you abide in me" (John 15:4 ESV). Jesus goes on to say if we abide in him, we "will bear much fruit" (John 15:5). He doesn't say we might or we may bear fruit. He says we will. There is no question about it. The key is abiding in him. We must focus on him instead of our own tools and abilities.

My brother-in-law is an avid hunter. Every fall is hunting season, and he spends months scouting the forest surrounding his dad's land. Years ago, he learned a valuable lesson about hitting your target. It's a lesson many newbies miss. You don't focus on your sights, which are at the end of the shotgun barrel. You keep your eyes set on your target. It involves a shift in our natural tendency. A shift in perspective. But the payoff is huge.

Like those new hunters, our normal inclination is to look at what we can control. We see our own weapons apart from the Spirit. Even when we feel the nudge to do something for God, we try to predict what will happen or wonder what the results will be. But instead of seeing only what we have in our hands, God is asking us to concentrate on the Spirit. So how do we do this? What do we know about the Spirit, and how do we shift our focus to him?

If we dig into Scripture, we learn these truths about the Spirit:

- He guides us. (Acts 8:29)
- He testifies about Jesus. (John 15:26)
- He gives us strength. (Eph. 3:16)
- He confirms what is true. (Rom. 9:1)

When we live empowered by these truths and adjust our focus to see the Spirit's potential instead of our capabilities, it not only changes our lives, but can impact the lives of others as well. The effects cascade to those around us as they can see the work of the Spirit transforming our hearts and minds. They see the results too, as we're filled with love, joy, peace, patience, kindness, goodness, faithfulness, gentleness, and self-control. Even when we aren't aware of the ways we're making an impact, the influence remains.

And what's even more beautiful? God sees, right? He sees, and others see a change in us. In the same way his disciples spread the news of his resurrection with courage and resolve after Jesus ascended to heaven, we can exhibit courage and great resolve even when we don't fully see where things are going.

> We are one of the primary ways an invisible God makes himself visible to others.

We extend compassion to those who are hurting, even when it feels risky. We encourage each other and pray for each other, even when we don't think our prayers sound educated or effective. We continue believing and seeking him; and if we don't see the answer or outcome we hoped would come, we seek him more. We are one of the primary ways an invisible God makes himself visible to others. When we do these things, Christ's love is made complete in us (1 John 4:12).

Others see him because they see our devotion in the face of uncertainty. They see him because we continue to alter our perspective toward the truths we know instead of the responses we don't yet perceive.

The Answer We Know

After Don passed, we spent weeks watching his caretaker and various others remove his belongings from his house. My stomach felt like it was twisted in knots, and I grieved the man who used to greet us from his front porch each day. I wondered whether anyone else saw the value of his life as his possessions were taken and sold to strangers, one by one.

Chris and I still have a lot of unanswered questions about our neighbor. But there are many things we do know, and we find comfort remembering them.

We know God called my husband to reach out to Don. He was completely alone after his dad passed, and he needed a friend. More than a friend, he needed a believer in his life who would point him toward God's truth.

We also know Don's heart was softening toward the church community. After years of staying away because of previous hurts, he was making friends with followers of Christ. Whether he was aware of it or not, his presence at the study made an impact. People noticed Don, and they saw the boldness Chris showed in extending an invitation to someone who was resistant. They saw that God is working even through the noes we receive. He's working during the moments we feel opposition and discouragement and in the moments we're not sure whether we're making a difference.

Most of all, we know Chris was obedient. And because he was obedient, his focus shifted from being self-empowered to Spirit-empowered. In Luke 10, an expert of the law tried to test Jesus, asking what he needed to do to inherit eternal life.

> He answered, "'Love the Lord your God with all your
> heart and with all your soul and with all your strength
> and with all your mind'; and, 'Love your neighbor as
> yourself.'" (Luke 10:27)

Even when he didn't see any indication that God was working and moving in Don's heart, my husband loved his neighbor. Even when he wasn't sure if his invitations would ever be accepted, he continued to step forward in faith. For months, he invited Don to church not sure if he would ever say yes. Until one day, he finally did.

This acceptance may have seemed small to some, but to us it was huge. It meant that when we step forward and do what God is asking us to do, he moves in ways only he can. Even when it doesn't seem like anything is happening. Even when it appears as though nothing has changed.

Each "no" led to a "yes." And the "yes" was our goal. The "yes" was everything.

In watching my husband take a step when he was unsure what the outcome would be, I was encouraged to do the same. I messaged our pastor's wife a Bible study I'd felt called to lead for months, but had been putting off. I began to reach out to others despite being introverted and hesitant about how they'd respond. I realized we never know how much time a person is going to have, and we should seize the opportunities we have to show kindness and compassion. I learned that sometimes loving others well means stepping outside of what feels comfortable. It means extending grace and empathy instead of assuming I know what someone is going through. When we do these things, others see Jesus because the Spirit is moving. The more we follow his leading, the more our lives become a living example of his power. They may not know what they're witnessing at the time or why our lives are different, but they're drawn to it.

A decision to follow Jesus is never in vain. Even when we don't know the end of the story. Even when we're not sure whether our prayers were answered. Our God is far bigger than the things we do or don't know. And as much as we loved our neighbor and wanted to see his heart transformed, God loved him even more. He loved him more than we could imagine.

When we make the choice to trust God even when we're unsure of the outcome and obey him even when we face doubt, lives are changed. A small act of kindness can be a big arrow pointing others toward God's character. People notice the way we live and the love we have for others. They see how we care about the person everyone else overlooks. They see the attentiveness we show to those who need help.

> A small act of kindness can be a big arrow pointing others toward God's character.

The act of remaining in the vine that Jesus speaks of in John 15 is a constant process. It is a daily decision to shift our perspective and stay focused on the next step God asked us to take instead of trying to predict the aftermath.

Instead of asking ourselves:	We ask ourselves:
How is this going to turn out?	Is this something God is asking me to do?
Can I control the outcome?	Can he do the heart work/the miracle?
What will this cost me?	Will my obedience point others to Jesus?

If we're Spirit-empowered instead of me-empowered, then we can know with certainty that regardless of what we see, God is in it. Even if we're anxious or unsure, we can take the next step he is asking us to take. Why? Because there are people who, like Don, have spent their lives running from God. When they think of God, they don't picture someone who gave up his own life to save them. They don't picture someone who would go to any lengths to have a relationship with them. They see those who have hurt them. They see people who proclaimed the name of Jesus but were far from him in their actions and the way they lived their lives. A name that is beautiful to us has been associated with hurt to these souls who have no idea who he is. But God is reaching out to them through you and saying, "Show them who I really am. Show them what I'm really like."

Our job is not to try to find the final result or ending. Our job is to do what God is asking us to do, and to be confident that he will do the rest. We believe the Guide who knows the way, and we shift our focus and questions toward the truths we know about him instead of the numerous detours, rocks, and bumps along the path.

Each time we look to him instead of our own limitations, a transformation is taking place. It takes time. As a matter of fact, the change lasts an entire lifetime, and we may not always see it while it's happening. But we can be sure he's working, even when we don't see an immediate outcome. When we choose to love in the name of Jesus, the ending will always be beautiful. And at a moment when we may least expect it, we'll see the evidence we crave.

Adjusting Our Lens

1. Are there areas in your life where your focus is on final destination, but God may want you to simply take the next step? What do you think that next step might be? Pray about it and write down the answer you receive. Go through the exercise

outlined in this chapter and ask the questions to determine if you are self-empowered or Spirit-empowered. Then, tell another believer you trust and commit to taking that next step, whatever it may be. Even if it's simply inviting someone over for dinner.

2. Has your vision become obscured in the ascent? Do the bleak circumstances or lack of answers around you keep you from seeing God? Spend some time thinking about one of the first aspects of God's character that drew you to him. His love? His steadfastness? Find a Scripture corresponding with that truth about him and meditate on it.

3. What does Jesus mean in John 15:4; and how can we remain in him, even when we can't see the final destination? What impact do you think remaining in him would have on your faith and those around you?

4. Spend some time thinking about a point in your life when another person impacted your faith in a personal way. What was it about their walk that made an impression on you? Do you think they were aware of it?

2

Looking Past Our Expectations

If we want to see God move, we have to be expectant. We have to keep our eyes open and be watchful. But the airport is probably the last place I would expect to see him. I realize that may sound negative, but let me explain. Not only am I a mom, I am also the queen of predicting worst-case scenarios. And airports? They're screaming with possibilities of things to go wrong. Delays, screaming babes on planes, turbulence—you name it. When my oldest son was two years old, we flew to visit my parents in South Carolina. Our growing family had just made our second cross-country move in five years, and my husband was working to get our new home ready. In order to give him time and space to refinish floors, Jaden and I flew south. Panic over flying without my calm support system surfaced a few days before we left, so I hashed through numerous what-ifs in my head.

What if the altitude caused him to get a headache? What if he cried nonstop and everyone on the plane glared at us the whole time? What if he wouldn't take a binky or a bottle to help regulate the pressure on his ears?

In the weeks leading up to the trip, I made every possible preparation. I packed the diaper bag with toys, a DVD player, and several movies to keep him entertained. I lined the inside pockets with fresh binkies and made sure we had supplies to warm a bottle. Everything was in order, and I felt sure we were equipped for whatever might happen.

But guess what? My son still screamed. Although most of the flight went well, during the last twenty minutes, he decided he'd had enough. I put his DVD player away after a glaring look from the flight attendant, who reminded me of their descent safety regulations. At that point, nothing I said or did made any difference to Jaden. He was inconsolable, and I felt like crying right along with him.

In the end, my best and worst predications about the flight couldn't control the outcome. Even if I'd worried more and made myself sick trying to foresee the future, it wouldn't have made a difference.

While my worst-case-scenario type thinking can certainly make me ready for things that may or may not happen, it can also blind me to the good happening all around. And if I'm honest, this invisible, protective barrier I put around me often manifests itself in my relationship with God as well. Instead of expecting God's best, I ask him to protect me from the worst.

Do you see a problem here? By attempting to protect myself from circumstances that usually never happen, my capacity to experience joy or even fully experience his blessings becomes limited. Tension and stress become my norm, making everyone around me stressed too. And by hyper-focusing on predicting the problems in the future, it becomes impossible to enjoy what's taking place right here, right now.

Although it's unlikely that any of us will completely let go of our expectations, what if we held on to them a little more loosely? What if we shifted our thinking in the way we approach the unknown? Instead of expecting trouble to arise, what if we moved forward with confidence that God will act out of his goodness and mercy? He wants to surpass our greatest hopes, but we have to let go of what we think will happen. Even if it's just a little at first.

Whether we come to God with a long list of requests or we come simply desiring protection, here's what we need to understand: God knows what we need even better than we do. He sees the complete story, while we see a word or a sentence at best.

Proverbs 15:3 tells us, "The eyes of the LORD are everywhere, keeping watch on the wicked and the good."

When we let him do the writing, amazing things happen.

A God Who Surpasses Our Greatest Hopes

My friend Christy knows what it means to relinquish our needs and expectations to God, but she also knows it isn't easy. She has firsthand experience with what it's like to hope for something, but face constant uncertainty about whether it will happen. For years, she prayed about the care of her brother, who is disabled from birth. Most of his life was spent under the care of her parents; but when their health declined, Christy felt God nudging her to invite them to move closer. Their home was on the other side of town, and Christy knew they needed her help.

With the support of Christy and her husband, her family moved into a condo about a mile away. It seemed like the perfect solution to their problems, but after a few months, they discovered there were thousands of dollars worth of structural issues with the condo. Christy questioned God and wondered why he would clearly lead her to move her parents closer, only to find a slew of problems that seemed impossible to overcome. Every time it seemed as though they were making headway in resolving the damage, another situation would arise.

We often question God when struggles come too, don't we? This is especially true when we are sure we were following his call and taking a step of obedience. We expect the confirmation from him to come in the form of abundance and blessing. While most don't say this out loud or admit it, many of us often think it. I have gone down this path of reasoning many times. And while God loves to bless us, he often takes us through a season that may seem like a detour. He is continually refining us, and what looks like a diversion may actually be an opportunity to shift our attention. Instead of focusing on the provision, we focus on the Provider.

While God's provision could look a hundred different ways, his unfailing ability to provide does not change. His heart for his children doesn't waver, and he knows each and every one of our needs.

At the time Christy and her family were facing multiple dilemmas with the condo they recently purchased, there was no way she could have known what God was doing. She kept praying and coming to him with a longing to see what his plans were, but for a difficult chapter of her life, she had no idea. It wasn't until a few years later, when Christy's parents were both gone, that she realized how God was working through each and every detail of her family's move.

When her mom passed, Christy was faced with a very difficult question: Where was her brother going to live? Although he needed a place where he could obtain assistance with things like transportation, he also wanted to maintain his independence. Christy knew he needed others around him, but also knew he desired a place of his own.

It just so happened that within months after Christy's mother's death, a one-of-a-kind community opened for people with disabilities. It was the only place like it in the nation. And because God was orchestrating these events even before Christy knew to pray about it, her brother's application to become a resident was accepted.

When recalling God's perfect provision, Christy said,

> The property the Arc Village was built on had been deeded the state fifty years earlier for the sole purpose of using for the handicapped. There it sat . . . for years until now . . . right when we needed it. But what if we hadn't moved my family in 2005? Would things have lined up the way they did? I don't know but I do know we went where God led us.[1]

Fifty years. Fifty years before this answer to prayer, God was orchestrating events and moving in hearts and minds so this village would later become a reality. Before Christy thought to pray about it or even think about it, God saw the need. And because he did, she had the privilege of joining 120 other residents at the ribbon cutting ceremony and heard about how far the Lord went to make this dream come true.

As it turned out, the family who helped make the Arc Village possible faced many obstacles during the planning and building of the facilities. Like Christy, there were probably days when they wondered if they'd heard God right and if he was still in control. But as they cut the ribbon and the crowd applauded, it was clear he was in each and every detail.

God did more than answer the prayers of Christy and many others. He surpassed anything they dreamed of. They couldn't conceive of such a provision, because this type of community had never been created. But God envisioned it. And he made it real.

Can you imagine if Christy had decided to move her family back across town when things got rough? Things may have turned out a lot differently. She may have never known about the Arc Village, because she would have been looking for a place in a different area. Her sensitivity to God's call and perseverance through the rough spots brought great reward.

Because of Christy's endurance and persistence in the face of obstacles, she was later able to see what God had planned for all those years. When problems arose, she continued praying and believing God was in control, even when she had no idea how things would work out. She shifted her focus from the problem to the One who knew the outcome.

When we take the same approach in our own lives, it looks something like this:

Instead of:	We:
Expecting trouble-free sailing	Expect God to be with us no matter what
Assuming God is punishing us	See struggles as part of God refining us
Thinking there is only one solution	Realize we serve a God of limitless possibilities

When Presumption Becomes a Problem

When we follow God into the unknown, our expectations of his grace must become greater than our dependence on an answer. Sometimes we're so focused on receiving a specific provision, we miss the bigger picture. God could be answering our prayers already, but we rush right past it because we expect the response to look a certain way. Then, when we don't see what we're looking for, we assume he hasn't heard us. We think he doesn't care about our needs or has abandoned us.

> When we follow God into the unknown, our
> expectations of his grace must become
> greater than our dependence on an answer.

While we may think presumption is harmless, David's words show it can be dangerous to our relationship with God. As a matter of fact, he asks the Lord to protect him from it. His words indicate he knew how far down a person could fall as a result: "Keep back your servant also from presumptuous sins; let them not have dominion over me! Then I shall be blameless, and innocent of great transgression" (Ps. 19:13 ESV).

If we dig into David's plea to the Lord, we see an awareness that conjecture or assumption about what God is doing can completely overtake a person's life and disrupt his or her intimacy with him. David, who is later called "a man after God's own heart," had experienced the harm of believing something that is far from the truth. He even goes so far as to say presumption can lead to "great transgression." This type of reasoning without all of the facts is not something David took lightly.

For the sake of clarification, let's define presumption in the context of faith. It's when we assume something about God as a result of our circumstances. For example, we may think he is absent because we are experiencing difficulties in our lives that seem insurmountable. If we look at some of the other psalms David wrote, we see he is no stranger to this type of thinking. However, there is a key element in David's reaction to his struggles that differentiates him from many others: he came to God.

Psalm 19 is written directly after David is delivered from the hand of his enemies. If we take a look at some of the history and the context of the preceding psalms, we see that David's son,

Absalom, had made false accusations against David and raised an entire army against him. Many of the psalms David wrote before God intervened are cries to the Lord for deliverance. We see him questioning where God is as he flees for his life and asking how long he will have to wait to be saved.

When I look at the earnest way David pours out his heart to the Lord, I find great comfort. Here is one of God's servants and a man he chose, but he still went through times when God felt distant or unreachable. During some of the most difficult seasons of his life, he asked why God was hiding his face from him. Seeing David's reaction shows that being honest with the Lord about our feelings does not send him running. As a matter of fact, if we look at the way most of these psalms of initial despair end, we see a change. We see a shift in the writer's perspective of God and the situation he is going through.

Psalm 13, which begins, "How long, O LORD? Will you forget me forever?" ends with him trusting in God's steadfast love and saying, "I will sing to the LORD, because he has dealt bountifully with me."

> Getting completely raw and honest with God brings a divine recognition of who he is.

When we look at these moments when David bares his soul before the Lord, we see that there's something about the process that causes him to counterpoint his humanness with God's sovereignty. What starts as a plea to be seen ends with recognition of God's unchanging character. Getting completely raw and honest with God brings a divine recognition of who he is.

David's position could have caused him to have a completely different reaction, though, couldn't it? He could have decided to turn his back on God. He could have run from him and decided to try to do things on his own. If I'm honest, this is often my reaction when life doesn't go according to plan. When my best-laid plans are crushed and my heart is hurting, sometimes I conclude God doesn't want to hear from me. Or I think my plan is better than his, and I run. Neither of these reactions gives me peace, though, which is what we see at the conclusion of David's psalm.

Instead of presuming God has left and walked away, David comes to him. Instead of saying, "Well, God hasn't answered my prayer, so there's no use in talking him," he talks to him openly as he would a friend. He gets real and confesses his intense human emotions. And in the process of doing so, he realizes something. God is still God. He hasn't left him before, and he's not going to leave him now.

Presumption doesn't disrupt our fellowship with God until we allow it to do so. Once we stop communicating with him and turn away, a greater darkness descends on our lives. We allow what we think we know to become greater than the God who knows all and sees the intricate details of our circumstances. We allow the solution we can't yet see to become greater than the truth we know. Although we may not admit it out loud, our actions show that we think our own plans for our lives are better than what God has in mind.

But when we come to God with a heart wanting a relationship and communication, he meets us exactly where we are. Even if our lives are complete chaos and we're not sure how we'll survive, he comes.

The next time we're facing troubles that seem unconquerable, let's use David's psalm as a blueprint. Let's expect God to hear us and answer us, even if our situation looks hopeless.

Using Psalm 13 as an example, David's cry to the Lord follows this design:

1. An honest admission to God about what he's feeling (vv. 1–2)
2. A call for God to open his eyes to truth and answer him (vv. 3–4)
3. A recognition of God's unfailing love (v. 5)
4. A decision to praise God despite his difficulties (v. 6)

When I follow this model of communication with God in my life, there's a change in my outlook. Instead of only seeing the mountain in front of me, I see the faithfulness of God. And it isn't because I try to avoid what I'm facing or belittle the problems that lay ahead, but because my focus shifts to the One who goes to battle with me. My open confession results in an awareness that he hasn't gone anywhere. He's right there with me, and he's fighting for me. Even when his armies remain unseen.

The View He Wants Us to See

In all of our family hikes up Mount Pisgah, our goal never changed. We wanted to get to the peak. Our burning muscles and tired feet didn't compare to the spectacular view spanning for miles around the mountain range. When I ran into rough patches on the trail and couldn't see very far up ahead, I trusted the guide in front of me, which was usually my dad or granddad. They'd navigated the path for years and knew how to reach the summit.

What if I had gotten deep into the forest and could no longer see the top of the mountain, so I decided to sit down and not go any further? What if I had assumed that because I could no longer see that radio tower that marked the pinnacle of our trek, it was no longer there? I would never have gotten to enjoy the reward for all of my exertion and witness the beauty God put on display for us to see. Instead of seeing a continuous expanse of valleys and vistas as far as my eyes could take me, I would have only seen the ground. My eyes would have remained locked on the dirt and the rocks along the trail.

Many times in life, this is what has happened to me. My expectation of what God is going to do prevents me from seeing what he *will* do, if I'll trust him. My assumption that he's not taking me anywhere I want to go keeps me from seeing the beautiful view he's trying to bring me up to see.

But every now and then, I get it right. I'm slowly learning to look up and see where God is trying to take me instead of constantly looking down. I'm seeing that the place he wants to take me is good and full of promise.

Remember all of my worst-case-scenario thinking and how far it got me? All of my preparations for my two-year-old's flight to South Carolina ended with him screaming at the top of his lungs for the last twenty minutes of our descent into southern heat and humidity.

Despite the fact that I wanted to buy everyone on the airplane a cocktail and disappear, God was working. My son's outburst produced an opportunity that wouldn't have come otherwise. While I wanted a well-behaved toddler and a tantrum-free flight, God wanted me to see what someone sitting in the seat in front of me saw. And what he saw was completely different from the way I viewed myself.

When the plane reached the terminal, all I wanted to do was get off. Our seats were near the front of the plane, and I rushed to grab the diaper bag, DVD player, and other things I'd brought in hopes that my worst nightmare wouldn't become a reality. I kept my head down as I carried Jaden on my hip toward the door. Then, I heard a man's voice behind me.

"You're doing a great job," he said. "Really. Keep it up."

As I turned around to say thank you, I saw the compassion in his eyes. And there was something else there too. Honesty. He meant what he said. He wasn't simply trying to make me feel better after the disastrous arrival. He wanted to affirm me as a mother. As a woman who was trying with everything she had to do the best for her kid.

Now, instead of rushing to get off the plane because of my son's outburst, I rushed to get off because of the tears building in my eyes. But first I gave the man a sincere "thank you." I walked to the door amazed that someone could be so kind and understanding after what I thought was the end of the world. I was completely blown away by his thoughtfulness.

Sometimes God doesn't give us what we want because he has something even better planned. God is lifting us up above the tree line to see what he sees, to see what others see, but we don't even realize it. Could the man on the plane have given me the compliment without the tantrum from my son? Sure. But it wouldn't have meant as much. This person saw me right in the middle of my mess, and he still encouraged me. And that made all the difference. It showed me that things could go the complete opposite of how I wanted, but what mattered the most would still be intact. I would still be the mom Jaden needed. I would still be the mom God wanted me to be.

I never expected to receive praise in my mothering abilities on my way off that flight. God saw a need I didn't even realize was there, and he filled it. I didn't get the perfectly behaved kid I wanted, but I received something even better. I received new confidence. My walk became a little straighter. My head lifted a little higher.

Surpassing Our Greatest Dreams

We serve a God who wants to surpass our greatest expectations, but in order to do so, we have to let go of some of the things we think we need. This doesn't mean we can't come to God with our desires, but we have to loosen our grip of control. When we do, our perspective changes. We're able to catch a glimpse of what he sees because we're not sitting our stubborn butts down on the trail, refusing to go any further. We're letting him guide. We're confident he sees what's ahead and will prepare us for it, even if it's not in our view yet.

Several years ago, I was preparing for my first writers' conference, and I wrote about some of my fears and apprehensions on my blog. My worst-case-scenario predictions were taking over my peace of mind again, and for once, I was honest about it. I'll never forget what an older, wiser writer, who had some life experience I didn't yet have, said to me in a comment after reading my piece:

> Go to the conference with a song in your heart, holding loosely to your dreams and tightly to his promises.
> Sounds like the two work against each other, but his promises go further than our dreams.[2]

Although it took me a season of disappointment and wrestling through my reader's statement to truly believe it, I now realize how right she was. I see that it's true not because I have everything I wanted, but because I know *him* more. The crazy thing is, the more I know him, the more conscious I am of how little I know. This realization is not something that scares me, but something that makes me want to praise him.

His plans for my life and yours go far beyond anything we can think or dream. His infinite wisdom and knowledge are beyond what we're able to conceive. If a God that great and limitless loves us and thinks of us more than we think of ourselves, don't you think we can lay our hopes at his feet? I promise you, they're safe there.

He will never trample them like a careless Father; he will exceed them in ways you never thought possible.

Adjusting Our Lens

1. Is there a prayer you've been hoping God would answer, but you don't see it yet? Could he be answering it in a different way you didn't anticipate?
2. In what ways have you experienced God answer prayer in an unexpected way, and how could you share this experience with others?
3. How does God give us evidence he's with us on this journey of life, even when we're not sure what he's doing?
4. Do you ever come to God like David did in Psalm 19 and tell him exactly how you feel? If so, did it change your perspective? If not, come to him right now and follow the blueprint he gives us with his Word.

3

Faith That Moves Our Feet Forward

"Sometimes I wish God would just give me a writing on the wall. Things would be so much easier that way, right?"

My friend's eyes welled up with tears as we sat at a local Asian restaurant, eating dinner and catching up on everything that had taken place over the past three months. She knew exactly what I meant. We both were facing some major decisions in our lives. For her, it was choices regarding her kids' schooling, and for me it was whether or not to continue writing and serving in certain areas of ministry. We were at a crossroads, experiencing the overwhelming confusion that comes when we think God is leading us down a certain path, only to face immediate roadblocks and detours.

I was in the middle of a season of rejection and waiting, and I longed for a clear sign from God that I should continue writing. Every time I thought he was giving me a green light to continue, doubt overtook me. Another "no" would arrive in my inbox, or a troll would stalk me on social media and rattle my faith. As my friend and I sat in the booth by the window on Tuesday night, we reasoned through things.

There was plenty on my plate to keep me occupied without writing. With two young kids and another on the way, it wasn't as though I didn't have valuable ways to devote my time. My family was a ministry and a calling in and of itself. Should I forgo writing for a later season?

But the more I thought about quitting, the more I knew I couldn't. Even though there wasn't a harvest in sight and the waiting continued, I knew I had to keep going. There was no writing on the wall or a contract from a major publisher. As a matter of fact, another rejection email arrived shortly after our conversation. And yet, there was something inside me that propelled me forward, even when there was no evidence of the elusive reaping.

Quitting wasn't an option for my friend or for me. So after some time commiserating, we encouraged each other. We spurred one another on in faith that God was still working, even though we couldn't see the outcome.

Our conversation reinforced a truth God has shown me over and over as I follow him: if we desire a faith that moves our faith forward, we have to shift our focus beyond what we can see with our eyes.

If our faith is determined only by visible results, it won't take us very far. But oh, how we long for a miracle story, don't we? We want God to move in a way where others will see his undeniable, inexplicable presence. We want them to witness what we have seen and experience the breathtaking awe we know he can create in hearts. I am certain God wants this too; but what if the catalyst that moves us forward goes beyond his mighty acts? What if it has less to do with what he does and more to do with who he is?

When Jesus called his first disciples, he didn't make some grand speech or turn water into wine to prove who he was. He simply said, "Come." And that was enough. There was something about him that was so electrifying, so pulling that these men couldn't say no to him. They didn't want to. They left everything they had and sacrificed their way of life, their families, and homes to follow someone they didn't even know. Why? What compelled them to do this?

If we look in Hebrews chapter 11, we're told faith is not the evidence of things seen, but not seen: "Now faith is the substance of things hoped for, the evidence of things not seen" (Heb. 11:1 NKJV). These disciples had the type of faith described here. Their trust in Jesus went beyond what they could see with their eyes and was based on a conviction they felt in their hearts. For them, the evidence wasn't based on a supernatural act. They were given a simple yes-or-no invitation. A call to a new way of life, completely different from what they knew. And their decision to follow him wasn't a mindless act, but an act of surrender.

So where does evidence of "things not seen" come from, and how does it apply to us today? Where do we look for confirmation that we're not just going on some wild goose chase? There has to be a solid foundation of truth to motivate us, or else we will eventually become weary and disillusioned. As I searched for the answer to this question, I found it interesting that this surrender to a higher power isn't limited to Christianity or even religion in general. As a matter of fact, if we look at the twelve-step programs adapted by Narcotics Anonymous and Alcoholics Anonymous, we see the same revelation.

The First Step We Must Take

My brother is an addict. I don't say that lightly or without feeling a string of pain as I write it. I've spent many nights coming to God with my cheeks wet from tears, pleading with him to show my sibling that his life has value. I've begged God to get his attention in such a way that turning back to a life of drugs will be unthinkable. So far, my prayers haven't been answered. My brother still lives shackled to a life of pain and chaos, and many of his loved ones are often victims on the path of destruction. But I continue to hope.

Daniel has been through several rehab programs. Some were court-mandated and others were Christian programs he attended with the encouragement of family and friends. Although each of the programs he attended was different and somewhat unique, I was struck by the similarities.

Whether you opt for a traditional NA program or a faith-based one, they begin with the same acknowledgment of the divine. The attendees must recognize that there is a higher power that is going to have to help them overcome their addiction. It doesn't matter if the person is a Christian, believer, agnostic, or atheist. This is step one, and this vital part of the process serves as a gateway to the rest of the journey toward freedom.

I always found this step intriguing and confounding at the same time, because the person is starting his or her journey by admitting a lack of control. Yes, he has a will. Yes, she has the ability to accept help or deny it. But the strength to press forward in the face of unrelenting opposition must come from somewhere else. It must come from God.

This admission of need isn't optional or a step that can be skipped over. It is crucial. And a person's failure to realize this truth is one of the reasons a large percentage of users relapse. They turn back to their own strength, and then realize it will get them nowhere.

However, there is also good news, and it's news we don't want to overlook. And it's this. As believers and followers of Jesus, we already have this power within us. The Holy Spirit lives in each of us, and he gives us what we lack: patience, courage, self-control, and a multitude of other attributes that enable us to be strong in the face of overwhelming odds. He's a fire burning inside us, and his flame is ignited by our belief and reliance on him.

The problem is, many of us live as though he isn't there. We walk around and do life like we're orphans instead of like daughters and sons who have a Helper. We make decisions and face the problems with the mindset that we have to do it all on our own instead of with his Spirit equipping us and giving us the courage and power we lack. If we look at some of Moses's encounters with God in Exodus, we see a similar pattern.

God set Moses apart and gave him a job impacting Israel's entire future. His actions would affect not only the nation he led, but also outsiders (Gentiles) who would later be adopted into Christ's eternal family. But Moses didn't believe God at his word. He doubted, again and again. He feared criticism from the Israelites and wanted proof it was God who was speaking to him. He asked for a miracle. A sign that couldn't be denied. Perhaps you can relate?

Often, we want a guarantee from God before moving forward and doing what he's asked us to do. So instead of acting out of obedience, we stall. We try to see into an unknown future or implore God for an indication that we're not going to be left empty handed.

Moses wanted the same type of guarantee, and was bold enough to ask for it. In an earnest plea to God, Moses said, "Please show me your glory" (Exod. 33:18 ESV). And you know what? God delivered. He honored Moses's request and showed up in such an incredible way that Moses had to cover his face when he returned to his people.

Here's the beautiful truth we often forget: if we are in Christ, we are living reflections of his glory. His transforming power isn't activated from outside, but within. Faith is activated not by seeing, but by doing, even when we don't know what the result will be.

This is not an invitation to self-sufficiency or a reason to think we can stand on our own. Our beauty comes from the Spirit alone and what he freely gives us. But you know what? I think many of us are like Moses. In one way or another, we're coming to God and saying, "Show me your glory." Even though his Spirit lives within, we want affirmation that he's there and that he cares. And many times, he gives it. But often, God wants us to exercise our faith in the unseen and take that first step forward.

> Faith is activated not by seeing, but by doing, even when we don't know what the result will be.

In our culture, we're taught that seeing is believing, right? Social media has trained our brains that if something isn't "liked" or approved with emoji-speed reactions, it didn't happen. However, Scripture shows us something quite different, and we have to retrain our brains to live in its truth. Instead of signs and miracles, our hope is in what we *can't see*. It's something that goes beyond this world and all its successes, failures, and accolades. "So we fix our eyes not on what is seen, but on what is unseen, since what is seen is temporary, but what is unseen is eternal" (2 Cor. 4:18). The Pharisees saw miracle after miracle performed, but they still didn't believe Jesus was the Messiah. While Jesus did use visible signs to prove who he was and draw others to him, their faith had to go deeper than a "here today, gone tomorrow" gratification from the supernatural.

As we move forward into the unknown, confident in truths we know of God, his Spirit moves and breathes new life into us. Even if visible proof that we're headed in the right direction isn't immediate, his Spirit will provide confirmation with our spirit. We'll find comfort right in the middle of a far-from-perfect situation.

When the Spirit gives us confirmation, we experience:

- A peace within, even if troubles surround us
- Conviction that we're going in the direction God desires, even if it isn't easy
- Alignment with God's truths and ways found in Scripture

These gifts the Spirit gives us aren't temporary. They are ours, even when struggles come and we have every reason to think we made the wrong decision.

Faith That Goes beyond Perfect Circumstances

As soon as my friend, Misty, heard about the opportunity to host an orphan from overseas, she knew they were going to do it. Shortly after she discovered the Open Hearts, Open Homes organization, she found a girl from Ukraine who needed a summer home. One look at the child's face was the only confirmation Misty needed. Not only did the ten-year-old girl look like a daughter, but they also shared a visual disability that my friend rarely talks about. Misty was certain this child was meant to be with her family.

There are a lot of risks involved with hosting an Open Hearts, Open Homes orphan, but none of them stopped my friend or her family. First, many children, such as the one they chose, have never experienced life outside an orphanage. They don't know what it means to be part of a family, ride a bike, or do day-to-day activities most of us take for granted. Also, many of the children are victims of trauma, and the effects of it often present themselves without any warning or time to prepare. There is also a language barrier, which is a huge challenge, even after studying common phrases and using apps like Google Translate.

Most of all, Misty's family didn't know what to expect. They didn't know if the girl they hosted would respond well to them or want to lock herself in a room the entire time. They didn't know if she would get along with their other kids and vice versa, or if they would constantly be breaking up fights, trying to maintain a calm environment. There were tons of questions and what-ifs. But in the end, they took a step into the uncertainty and said yes. Their desire to follow God's leading was bigger than their fear of the unknown.

> Their desire to follow God's leading was bigger than their fear of the unknown.

When their Ukrainian girl arrived, she was nothing but smiles. By the time they left the airport to bring her to their house, she was already showing affection and putting her arm around Misty. This openness and willingness to be loved was unexpected, but welcomed.

Even though the beginning of her visit went smoother than they had ever imagined, the next month was not easy. Over the next few weeks, they faced numerous difficulties. It was obvious their orphan came from a troubled past, and the results of her upbringing became more and more evident. Tears flowed often, and some afternoons were spent without leaving the house for fear of further upsetting a child who was already struggling to make sense of things.

After a month of staying with Misty's family, it was time to leave and return home to the orphanage. Some people wondered what good even came out of the visit since she was going back to the same life she left behind. Questions arose like clockwork, and some are still without answers. Would she find a permanent home? Would she return to the orphanage with a newfound confidence? Would the love she was shown and the memories made change her stride and, most of all, her life? Despite the questions, the overwhelming grief, and the empty space left in her heart, Misty knows they made the right decision.

Some of you may be asking, "How?" How does she know? Because they did what God asked them to do. Nothing more, nothing less. Even though everything about the visit didn't end tied up with a neat little bow, her family showed this little Ukrainian girl a love she'd never experienced before. She learned how to ride a bike and swim. She saw the ocean for the first time. Faith and the love of a God she never knew about were introduced to her, and she saw how he makes himself known through his written Word. She was part of a family and part of their lives, and even if it was only for a short while, the impact they made will last for the rest of her life.

Misty describes it like this:

> I didn't want to put her on the plane. It was hard hugging her with a final, "I love you." But the grief is worth it. I can't imagine not having known and loving her. So for the thousand happy moments, I'll take the grief. It is worth it. It's an honor to be a part of her story, a bridge to her future. I put her on that plane and I'm confident she knows she's loved.[1]

In James, we're told faith without works is worthless. Although Jesus's half-brother's statement may seem harsh, it serves as a warning that a complacent, stay-in-my-comfort-zone faith reflects a spirit that has become static and hard. "What good is it, my brothers and sisters, if someone claims to have faith but has no deeds? Can such faith save them?" (James 2:14).

> A healthy faith is a forward-moving faith.

Even though Misty and her family don't know what the future holds for them or the Ukrainian girl who made a permanent impact on their hearts, they know they were obedient to God's call. And despite all the loose ends and uncertainties, knowing they followed him is enough. A healthy faith is a forward-moving faith.

Forward-Moving Feet Require a Firm Foundation

Isaiah 7:9 tells us, "If you are not firm in faith, you will not be firm at all" (ESV). So, what makes our faith firm? How can we continue moving forward, even when we face overwhelming obstacles? Our faith must be grounded in what we know of God or our lives will become pure chaos when troubles come. And if we've been living on this planet for long, we know trouble always comes at some point, doesn't it? Sometimes it's after a chapter of harvest or blessings; but as Jesus warned his disciples, struggles are inevitable. If our circumstances, family life, financial security, or anything else becomes our foundation, we will have no direction or stability when the inevitable seasons of difficulty come.

To live our lives based on a faith that propels our feet forward, a firm foundation is critical. Stability that is based on something other than God's truths and our faith in them will send us into a dark abyss as soon as our feet start running. But the truth is, most of us want the happy result or ending. We want the friend with the diagnosis to find a miracle cure. We want the family member with the marriage that's in trouble to find restoration and healing. We want the orphan girl to find a permanent home with a family who will love her unconditionally.

A year ago, an invitation from my son helped me conquer a fear of heights. He challenged me to fumble my way through a four-story-high ropes course with him, and the opportunity to make memories with him was too good to pass up. However, once our harnesses were securely tightened and we made our way through the first set of obstacles, I made a costly mistake: I looked down. As the wobbly bridge I was crossing swayed back and forth, I wondered what possessed me to agree to an adventure that was about to make me lose my breakfast.

"Don't look down, Mom!" my son called as he looked back at me with a grin.

Yep, too late.

I stood there for a moment regaining my composure and learned a vital lesson. My son was right. Instead of looking at the ant-sized people moving around below, I needed to keep my eyes fixed on the rope in front of me. The ropes were affixed to metal beams that ran down on each side of the course into a concrete foundation. And because the foundation was secure, the course was secure. My harness was connected to another metal line directly above me as I moved across.

Many times, we make the same mistake I did while following my son across the rickety bridge. We look at our changing scenery instead of an unchanging God. We look at objects that are moving around us and become dizzied instead of keeping our eyes fixed on the truths we know of our Helper. The foundation to which our safety harness is attached turns out to be a cracked, crumbling mess instead of a secure slab of concrete.

So the next time we're temped to look at our changing environment, let's pace ourselves, repeating these truths. The truths will become our firm stepping-stones, each one firmly secured in the river that never runs dry. Let's walk together.

- Step One: Jesus Christ is the same yesterday, today, and forever. (Heb. 13:8)

- Step Two: His compassions never end. (Lam. 3:22)
- Step Three: He is sovereign and all knowing. (Isa. 40:13–14)
- Step Four: He loves us and has given us all we need through Jesus. (1 John 4:9)

Don't Miss the Little Miracles

After I met my friend for dinner that fall evening and we talked about wanting a sign from God, I kept writing. I didn't get the "yes" I wanted, and rejection letters still came; but after a few weeks, I received a note of encouragement. A reader reached out to me and shared how a blog post arrived in her inbox at just the right time. Her email came on a day when I was feeling discouraged, and I knew God was using this woman I'd never met to give me a push of motivation.

As I closed my eyes and thanked God for this woman's kindness, I felt him saying to me, "Abby, you are concerned with long-term goals and platforms, but I want you to see each and every reader as a person." I was convicted and inspired at the same time. I committed to praying for the readers who commented on my posts and corresponded via email. When had I forgotten the value of the individual? The angels in heaven rejoiced over one person coming to Christ, so why shouldn't I? Each reader was a miracle from God, and each one propelled me forward.

Then, several months after the note of encouragement, an invitation came. An editor of a popular Christian women's website wanted me to contribute to a 365-day devotional book. The offer was completely unexpected. I didn't even know this person looked at my website, let alone enjoyed what I wrote. The opportunity came when I was still wading through sleepless nights with my newborn girl and wondering if writing as a distant dream. With another nudge from God, I kept going and carving out a small amount of time each day to write.

When I saw my friend later in the year, she shared how God had guided her in the tough decisions she was facing as well. After several years attending a private Christian school, her kids were now homeschooling. A few phone calls with teachers made the choice clear for my friend, and she knew it was the right path. Her kids were now thriving at home and with extracurricular activities, and she was confident in her choice.

> Sometimes it isn't until we take shaky steps into the unknown that we see God's hand move.

Sometimes it isn't until we take shaky steps into the unknown that we see God's hand move. A faith that propels our feet forward isn't about the light or miracle in the distance. It's about the One who directs our steps.

We may question our course and wonder if he's even there, but if we keep our minds fixed on what's true and secure, we can keep going. Even when it's scary. Even when the road is rocky and gets a little windy along the way.

Although we may only know the first step to take, when we're obedient, he'll give us the next one. And once we take that first step, we'll begin to see the course he has already mapped out for us. We'll see that he knew the way all along.

Adjusting Our Lens

1. Is there an area of your life where you sense God asking you to step into the unknown? Perhaps it is in your church or your community. If there is, pray about it and talk to a believer you trust. Then, if you receive affirmation it's from God, commit to taking the next step.

2. Have you ever taken a step of faith you felt was prompted by God, but then hit roadblocks or detours? What do you think God was trying to teach you through the struggles you experienced?

4

The Treasure That Takes Us beyond This World

Sometimes we complicate the next step God wants us to take, when he simply wants us to take the one in front of us. We look for an alternate route or a way around his path, when he wants us to move forward. Even when the future is unknown. This is what I realized years ago.

One of my first experiences with moving into an uncertain future was over two decades ago at my college graduation. Goodness, that statement makes me feel old. The long line of square hats moved forward, tassels swaying back and forth, and I wondered how much the announcer would slay my last name. Since my graduating class had over 3,500 students, there were bound to be a few hiccups with pronunciation. Add to that the fact that my maiden name was German and was not spelled in a way that followed English phonetic rules. I knew I was doomed.

The succession inched forward, with each walk across the stage bringing applause that echoed through the colosseum.

When the podium stretched out before me, I said a prayer, hoping I wouldn't trip on the steps leading upward. The announcer said something that was not even close to my name, and jokes about it followed for weeks. But you know what? At that point, it didn't matter. My diploma was in my hands. It was a visible reward for four years of studying, tests, and hard work. My efforts paid off, and the "real world" beckoned.

Isn't it gratifying when we see immediate results for a job well done? Or perhaps we've been working toward a goal for years, and we finally reach the finish line. It satisfies us to see tangible proof we've hit the mark.

When that diploma entered my hands, I didn't realize I was entering a world where palpable rewards for achievement would be fewer and further between. My life stretched out before me like a blank canvas. But even at the crossroads between the past and the future, there are some things that remain the same.

For one, noticeable payoffs drive me. You too? We live in a results-driven world, and whether we're trying to lose weight or achieve the next rung on the career ladder, we want to know when we've accomplished something worth celebrating. Wouldn't it be nice if someone handed us a diploma or a certificate of achievement for each victory? We could hang them on our refrigerators next to our kids' artwork.

God knew this inward desire for reward and recognition when he created us. The writer of Ecclesiastes says,

> What do workers gain for their toil? I have seen the
> burden God has laid on the human race. He has made
> everything beautiful in its time. He has also set eternity

in the human heart; yet no one can fathom what God
has done from beginning to end. (Eccles. 3:9–11)

There it is in verse nine: the desire to be seen and rewarded. But do
you see the tension between what is temporary and what is eternal
in this passage? There is a yearning for a fulfillment beyond this
life, but we don't adequately understand it. We try to fill it with
things of this world, but are left empty.

When doing a word study on this passage, I found it interesting that the Hebrew word for eternity, *ha-ʿolam*, can also be
translated "the world."[1] We either have to choose one or the other,
don't we? In the context of the passage, it's clear the author was
referring to eternity, but the double meaning of the Hebrew word
illustrates the dichotomy between the two motives that can fill
our hearts.

When Short-Term Benefits Beckon

Often, I'm tempted to trade long-term gain for short-term victories. There have been times when I thought God wasn't listening to
my prayers or was holding back on me, and I decided to take matters into my own hands. Usually, it didn't end well. Over and over
again, he's shown me how an investment in something that lasts is
far more valuable than an instant, fleeting moment of gratification.

A perfect example of this truth happened to our family ten
years ago. At the time, I didn't see much value in thinking ahead.
Although I thought I made decisions with long-term benefits and
consequences in mind, if I'm honest with myself, I didn't. I wanted
a perceivable answer in a short time frame. After waiting what felt
like forever for a blessing my husband and I sought, we decided
it was better to make things happen on our own. So instead of
waiting on God's timing, we made a hasty decision that impacted
our lives for the next decade. And while the outcome wasn't

completely catastrophic, we faced some difficult times because of the choice we made.

We had been married less than a year when we moved cross-country to pursue a job opportunity for my husband. Two thousand miles stood between us and any family or friends, and culture shock hit us hard. Our new city in northern Utah was vastly different from South Carolina, and each day was both an adventure and a challenge. I tried to view our new life through the lens of the former, but there were days when I wanted to jump the next plane back to my southern home.

Within a month of our arrival, the temporary housing in our furnished, company-paid apartment expired, and we had to find a place to live. Fast. Finding suitable housing that would allow us to rent month-to-month and accommodate pets did not prove easy. We had two dogs, and they were a nonnegotiable part of the deal.

After a few days, our realtor found a place where we could live until we were able to sell our house back in South Carolina. We were thrilled. That is, until we saw it. Jaime tried to prepare us, telling us the home needed a little TLC, but her words were an understatement. When I pulled into the driveway, I wondered if there were squatters living there. Paint peeled off the wood-paneled exterior and the front porch sagged from wear. The yard was so overgrown you could barely find the walkway leading up to the steps.

As I walked to the front door, I wanted to be grateful for this home that God clearly provided. But I felt stuck in limbo. One home sat on the other side of the country, unsold and still costing us money, and this one clearly wasn't going to be our permanent residence. Neither Chris nor I had the time to invest in making this house a suitable place to live. The work it needed was extensive and costly. But it was clear we were going to have to at least do some major cleaning. When I opened the front door, layers of dust greeted me.

A month after we moved into the rental property, we were no more thrilled about it than when we arrived. Our home in South Carolina still hadn't sold, and our patience waned. Every showing brought complaints about the layout, the size of the rooms, and other issues we couldn't fix. We decided to call our bank about financing options. When we discovered that by pulling a few strings we could purchase a home in Utah without selling our other one, we couldn't restrain ourselves. Let me rephrase that. We didn't restrain ourselves. We called our realtor the next day and asked her to start showing us properties in our favorite neighborhood, the East Bench. She was ecstatic and began searching her inventory immediately.

Less than two months after we purchased a home on the East Bench, our house in South Carolina sold. We quickly realized the absentmindedness of our decision not to wait. Not only would we have had a considerable down payment to put toward the property we purchased, but we would have been able to consider others in a higher price range. And although God provided our needs even after I quit my full-time job to stay home with our first child, there were definite consequences to our hastiness. Several years later when we moved again and needed to sell the house in Utah, we were unable to do so. The housing market had not recovered from the Fanny Mae crash and all the repercussions that came with it; and since we had not made a down payment, we still owed more than we could make off the property.

Sometimes when we decide to rush God's plan for our lives and take control, he lets us do it. He gives each of us free will to live our days here on earth and make our own choices. We can decide whether to wait for him to act or carve our own way when he doesn't move on our timeline. When we trade long-term rewards for short-term conveniences, there will always be consequences.

> When we trade long-term rewards for short-term conveniences, there will always be consequences.

We may not see the consequences right away. It could take years or even a lifetime for us to recognize what our impulsiveness cost us. But eventually, it will come to light. Why? Because whether we realize it or not, everything we say, do, or achieve in this life either contributes to the temporary realm or the eternal realm. The elements that contribute to the eternal are as simple as they are profound. They're also easy to remember: faith, hope, and love. "And now these three remain: faith, hope and love. But the greatest of these is love" (1 Cor. 13:13). Sound overly simplified and inapplicable to our every day? It isn't. Here's how each of these elements is essential in day-to-day life:

Faith: Our perseverance in periods of waiting contributes to our faith. As our faith grows, so does our hope.

Hope: Our focus on the One who is ultimately in control and choice to trust his timing boosts our hope.

Love: Our love for him and our deep-seated knowledge that he loves us more than we can fathom keeps us devoted to following him no matter what.

Each component of the life Paul describes works together and is indispensable. Individually, they are useless. Faith without hope leads to despair, and hope without love leads to uselessness.

God isn't as concerned with the temporary comforts and achievements of this lifetime as he is with the eternal condition of our souls. Yes, he wants to bless us and care for us as a Father would look after his child. He wants to fill us with a joy so unexplainable we can't imagine a life apart from him. He knows our needs, and he is attentive to them. But ultimately, he's looking at how our actions and inactions affect the person he's molding and transforming each day to reflect his image. While we look at today, he's looking at our future.

Most of us don't spend much time thinking about death in our day-to-day lives. Unless we're facing a terminal illness or have a close loved one who is, our mortality doesn't impact our decisions much. But the fact is, when we breathe our last breath, the three elements Paul mentioned are what will remain. They are the attributes of our daily walk that will stand when everything else fades.

So how can we live with the eternal nature of our spirit in mind? How should this knowledge change the way we go through our days? Is it even possible to live this way?

This question is one I determined to answer. And the more I searched, the more I realized how possible it is.

Short-Term Races versus Long-Term Heart Lessons

Nothing shows me the importance of leaving a legacy of faith and commitment to things that matter more than parenting. I'll never forget the year my firstborn entered his first Pinewood Derby race. He was a Tiger in our local Cub Scouts pack, and to say he was excited would be an understatement. For weeks, he devoted time to the design and completion of his car. He drew out his specs on paper for the wood shop, buffed his axels, and taped off his car to be painted. If the work was within his five-year-old hands' ability to complete, he did it. The rules for the race explicitly stated that the scout was supposed to do the majority of the work himself, so while we guided him with what steps to take, we kept our hands off unless necessary for his safety.

When we arrived at the church on race day, I was surprised to see a row of cars that were clearly not done by kids. The intricacy of the detail and flawless performance of some of the racers soon made it clear that the first rule had been strategically overlooked by most of the parents. My first reaction was to feel horrible for my son, who had no chance of winning the race. To be honest, I felt like we'd failed him. Here were these other kids flying past him on the track with the help of their dads' master craftsmen skills.

But the more I observed my son, the more I noticed something. Jaden was still having fun. He was full of joy because he finished the work all on his own, and now he was seeing the results of his efforts. When he came in first place in one run, he was elated. It didn't matter that he didn't receive a trophy or join the top three in the final battle. His achievements were as simple as they were important: he made a car, he entered his first race, and every success was his because the work was his.

Each year, my son's abilities to craft a killer racecar became better. Last year, his results qualified him for his first district race. He's seen the direct correlation between long-term commitment and long-term rewards. Those skills and dedication to the project at hand? Those are lessons that will stay with him for years to come. And even though there were times I wanted my husband to jump in and take over the building, I've learned a few things as well. The long-term benefits of commitment to our work far outweigh the short-term satisfaction of an undeserved win.

When we parent a child, we aren't simply looking at the exterior. No mother who knew what was best for her child would look at him and say, "Well, since you haven't learned what I'm trying to teach you in the past five minutes, I'm giving up." It's not logical. We know our kids are acquiring new knowledge and developing each day, so their reaction to a challenge today could be vastly different than what it will be a few years down the road.

> The long-term benefits of commitment
> to our work far outweigh the short-term
> satisfaction of an undeserved win.

We're raising tiny humans who will hopefully one day be functioning adults in society. In the same way, God is raising up followers who will one day meet him face to face. He isn't just looking at our today or our week. He's looking at who we're becoming. He's viewing the perpetual story he's writing through our lives and the lives of those around us. When we become too preoccupied with the small and momentary, we miss the big. We miss being part of something far greater than ourselves because we're obsessing over a comfort that will be here today and gone tomorrow.

Now, I'm not asking you to give up your house, apartment, or job. I don't think God is either. But I do think if we were all sitting together having a conversation, he'd be asking us, "What is keeping you from me? What is the one thing hindering your soul from freedom and transformation?"

Can you answer that question? If Jesus were sitting here right now, what would you tell him? And most importantly, would you give it to him?

The Cost of Freedom

Jesus was known for getting to the heart of the matter. Throughout the Gospels, he referred to the "one thing" in his interactions with followers, other Jews, and seekers of the truth. For example, in his famous interaction with Martha in Luke 10, Jesus tells her "only one" thing is needed. Sometimes, his teaching was received with a heart longing for change. And other times, a lost soul counted the cost as being too much.

If we want to enjoy the full, complete life God has for us, we have to believe what he is offering us is better than anything the world can give us. Sometimes, this truth is too difficult for us to believe. Such was the case for a rich man who wanted to know the cost of eternal life. Even though he followed the letter of Jewish law since he was a boy, Jesus said he lacked "one thing" (Mark 10:21).

But before telling him what that one thing was, Mark gives a look into Jesus's heart toward this man. "Jesus looked at him and loved him" (Mark 10:21). Can we stop right here for a moment? Because I'm afraid our tendency is to rush right past those words when they hold the key to everything we're discussing. Jesus looks at this man and his desire is for him to have the best life possible. He speaks not out of wanting to withhold something from him, but out of love. Out of a yearning to give him fullness of joy and freedom. But as this man listens to Jesus, he doesn't really hear him. What the rich man hears is "lack, lack, lack," when what Jesus actually wants to give to him is "full, full, full."

> "'One thing you lack,' he said."

He knew what was keeping this man from transformation and freedom. For us, it may be something different. But whatever it is, trust me, he sees it. We can try to hide it or pretend it isn't holding us back, but we can't fool God. And he will use whatever means necessary to prompt our hearts toward change. However, prompting is quite different from forcing, and he will never force us to do anything.

> Go, sell everything you have and give to the poor, and
> you will have treasure in heaven. Then come, follow me.
> (Mark 10:21)

At this point, it's over for the rich man. His face falls. He walks away sad and dejected. He can't see past his temporary wealth to realize the greater riches Jesus is offering him. His blindness prevents him from knowing the truth, and he settles for short-term comfort instead of sharing an eternal table with the King of Kings.

Can you imagine the disappointment Jesus felt? This is not what he wanted for this man, and it's not what he wants for us. And yet so often, we have the exact same reaction this man did. God extends his hand with treasures beyond what our dreams can contain, but we decide to stick with what's in front of us. The safe. The comfortable. The riches we see.

What would happen if we truly believed God was offering us something better than short-term wealth or prosperity? Something better than temporary success? I believe it would change the way we lived. I believe we would be able to hold onto the achievements, accolades, and commodities of this world more loosely because of a change in our perspective. Our lives would be happier and more content because instead of looking at the momentary blessings in our days as crucial to our satisfaction, we'd look at them as gifts to be shared and, one day, left behind. When our faith in God's path for us is greater than our faith in today, a whole new world opens up before us.

Jesus describes it to his disciples like this:

No one who has left home or brothers or sisters or
mother or father or children or fields for me and the
gospel will fail to receive a hundred times as much
in this present age: homes, brothers, sisters, mothers,
children and fields—along with persecutions—and in
the age to come eternal life. (Mark 10:29–30)

Jesus doesn't try to sugar coat the fact that our lives won't be perfect after we decide to follow him. There's no doubt we'll face difficulty. But we'll also find blessing, reward, and purpose. And most importantly, we'll find redemption and renewal.

> When our faith in God's path for us is greater than our faith in today, a whole new world opens up before us.

A New Perspective

So what does this new perspective look like? How does thinking about the infinite nature of God and our souls impact the way we live life each day? To discover the answers to these questions, I had to walk through some hard life lessons.

When my husband and I purchased our house in Utah ten years ago, I couldn't see beyond the mess that surrounded us. I thought we needed a place to call our own because everything else seemed foreign. I longed for an anchor, and I thought a home would give us that. I thought it would give us stability and security. I didn't realize how much God wanted to bless us and give us the desires of our heart, but we needed to allow him to do it in his timing.

Since we didn't wait for him, we ended up carrying two mortgages for seven years. After we moved again and were unable to sell the Utah house, we decided to rent it. But the rent wasn't enough to cover our monthly payment, and many seasons brought costly upkeep and repairs. Each month, we had to rely on God's provision more than ever and trust him to supply our needs. We learned what it meant to be good stewards of the resources God gave us and to live prepared for emergencies instead of being blindsided by them.

Although there were weeks when we were financially strapped and stressed beyond belief, the growth and the life change we experienced during those seven years were invaluable. We saw what it meant to look beyond today because we had to. We saw that God does offer us gifts far greater than the fleeting comforts of this life, and we can enjoy them regardless of where we work, live, eat, or lay our heads.

If I were to sit with you over coffee today and share what this new perspective looks like, here's what I'd say:

Short-Term View Tells Me:	Long-Term Hope Tells Me:
If I can't have this, I won't be happy.	Momentary blessings bring momentary happiness, but the joy God gives is mine to keep.
If God doesn't deliver this want/need right now, he never will.	God's timing is perfect, and he will give when I am ready to receive.
Having this desire/blessing/gift will make me secure.	My security is not dependent on any temporary thing. It is in Christ alone.

(Side note: none of these short-term views are true.)

During those seven years of carrying two mortgages, my husband and I often became restless. We tried more than once to sell our house in Utah and even discussed moving back there. But then we realized something. It wasn't having a perfect home or even an ideal community that made us happy. Yes, having a good church home was a major part of our ability to thrive, but we could be content exactly where we were. We could enjoy God's abundance and grace all around us and thank God for what he'd already done. And once we stopped trying to rush the answer to our prayer, God opened the door. The housing market climbed, and we were able to sell our house in Utah.

Don't get me wrong; I still love to decorate and watch HGTV. Chip and Joanna Gaines are welcome to come transform our house at any time. But the more I invest in the temporary fixes and upgrades, the more I realize there will always be more to do.

On the other hand, when I invest in a relationship, build character, or share the love of Christ with someone, something timeless happens. These things are priceless. Their value goes beyond the realm of the here and now and into a place we can't yet see.

I know none of us can give up those momentary gifts completely. I don't think God expects us to. However, I do think he'd like us to see them for what they are: brief and fleeting. Luxuries we should hold with open hands. When we do, we can truly live. When we remember the brevity of our time here, we can make decisions that will create a beautiful legacy and pave the way for generations to come.

Adjusting Our Lens

1. There are three areas in which we often crave short-term results: work, family, and church life. What are your immediate goals in each area? Write them down. What are your long-term goals? Write these down too and see if they correspond to the short-term ones. If they don't, you may need to reevaluate and ask yourself, "What am I ultimately trying to achieve in this area?"

2. Ask yourself, "Am I investing more of my time in things or in people?" While there's nothing inherently wrong with having things, when *things have us,* the result is our hearts aren't aligned with God's. We see this with the rich man in Mark. While people may disappoint us at times, investing in relationships and people always yields a greater benefit than investing in things.

5

Hope in God's Plan or Our Own?

No word on earth gives you a clearer picture of the brevity of our time here than this one: cancer. It's a word that brings into focus everything important in this life—and all the rest of it seems to fade into the distance like the clouded background in a portrait.

My vision blurred after reading the text once, twice, then three times. Perhaps the sentences across the screen would somehow change with repetition. Maybe my brain wasn't fully awake yet, and with time the message would make sense. But the truth wouldn't go away, and my mind wouldn't be fooled. That ugly, dread-filled word still lingered there in white against the blue background, refusing to change. It was the third time my husband and I had heard it in the past year. The next few hours would be filled with questions without answers, silent pleas without explanation, and waiting. We knew another surgery was eminent, and this time the person in the OR would be Chris's dad.

It just didn't seem right. Several months ago, the person with the tumor was my mother-in-law. An extensive operation brought her in and out of the hospital for months, and she was finally beginning to feel like herself again after difficulty eating and digesting food. Now it was my father-in-law. This was the family we'd prayed over for more than a decade. The family who had been baptized in the Potomac River the previous summer. We stood at the boat ramp and watched, hearts filled with pure joy despite the sultry heat and complaining kids. Two women sang gospel music in the background while one strummed a guitar, and my mind went to all the times we'd hoped for my in-laws to dedicate their lives to Christ. Now, here we were. And it was beautiful. For a few seconds, anyway.

But then there was a turn. Over the next few months, texts and phone calls brought news none of us saw coming. People rarely foresee the seasons they'd rather skip over, do they? And while I believe it's our faith that can get us through those chapters of life where we'd rather burrow our heads into a dark cave and ignore our existence altogether, part of me questioned. Part of me asked, "Why now?"

Most of us don't voice a belief that new life in Christ should be full of trouble-free, open roads without bumps or detours. But sometimes we think it, whether consciously or subconsciously, don't we? Deep down, there's a place in our hearts screaming for things to be made right. When the diagnosis comes or a loved one passes far too soon, we feel our souls yearning, crying out, "It's not supposed to be this way, God!" And we're right. It isn't. We were never supposed to be separated from the One who created us, knows us, and planned our days before we were a glint in our mother's eye. We were supposed to exist in continual communion with him. And even though Christ's blood covers those of us who believe, we still live in a fallen world ruled by an enemy who never quits.

So what does this enemy want? What is his goal? Quite simply, his goal is to distract. His purpose is to use any means possible to keep us from fulfilling our God-given purpose, make us turn our backs on God, and stop pursuing a relationship with him. Pain and suffering are one of the many ways he does this; and sadly, it often works.

Why is this tactic so effective? Because for most of us, there are some types of hardship we look at and plainly say, "I don't see what good could possibly come from this." We may not see the point in even attempting to look for it. It could be an illness or a sick child. It may be a financial burden or loss. Perhaps it's abuse or neglect. Most of us don't look at these situations and see how God's light could penetrate the darkness. Those elusive silver linings don't seem to apply in these conditions. Instead, we want to know why. We want an explanation. And while these are normal reactions, it's important to realize that God never intended for us to live with the weight of these circumstances. This world is a far cry from the one he desired; and although we live with the pain of what's lost now, one day he will restore everything. But until then, a shift needs to occur in how we view suffering.

> Most of us view trials through the filter of punishment instead of viewing them through the lens by which we should regard every aspect of our lives: God's love.

We equate gifts and blessings with God's love. But hardship? We see that as discipline or negligence. We may think God dropped the ball all together or took the day off while our loved one suffers. He stopped listening to our prayers when our friend's marriage fell apart. But our Father wants us to look beyond what we're going through to where he's taking us. Most of us view trials through the filter of punishment instead of viewing them through the lens by which we should regard every aspect of our lives: God's love. Yes, the view may be obscured by obstacles right now. This is why we need him. This is why we must extend our hands instead of clenching our fists.

If we look at Scripture, painful seasons are not portrayed as a curse from God. As a matter of fact, there is an abundant harvest to be reaped from them. But this yielding of fruit doesn't come from hiding. It doesn't come from our attempts to skip over the difficult stuff. It comes from a decision to "glory in our sufferings" (Rom. 5:3). When we do this, the reward is manifold:

> because we know that suffering produces perseverance;
> perseverance, character; and character, hope. And hope
> does not put us to shame, because God's love has been
> poured out into our hearts through the Holy Spirit, who
> has been given to us. (Rom. 5:3–5)

A look at Merriam-Webster tells us "glory," when used as a verb, means, "to rejoice proudly." What a minute. Rejoice proudly in the trenches of life we would rather avoid altogether? Why would anyone do this?

I have to admit, the first few times I read these verses in Romans my reaction was to ask, "Do people really do this?" Perhaps you've been there too. The Bible is not simply a collection of stories, but a source of truth we want to apply to each day. In this context, it's natural for it to feel like wading through mud from time to time. It's okay to say, "God, this is hard." Those moments when we get into trouble are when we *do* skip over the difficult stuff and choose to stick with the milk. When we decide we'd rather live on our own terms than taste what God has for us.

When we live the way Paul describes and choose to worship despite what is going on around us, something amazing happens. We see that the faithfulness of God transcends our circumstances. Not because he always gives us what we want or because he makes us understand every detail. It's not because of what's happening on the outside, but what he's doing on the inside. He's changing our hearts. And what we see is this. God's faithfulness is not a result of what he does, but who he is.

> God's faithfulness is not a result of what he does, but who he is.

It is impossible for him to be anything *but* faithful. It's against his nature to do anything that isn't perfect, holy, and just. So when crisis and chaos hit, which they inevitably will at some point, we can know for certain it isn't because God's character has changed. And we can be sure he is still working, even if we can't see it yet.

If we're going to see him, though, we must look for him in the midst of the suffering instead of merely waiting for the deliverance from it. We must learn he's as present in the dark valleys as he is in the light.

Finding God in the Darkness

My friend Lisa has seen God's presence in those moments we hope we'll never face. She's witnessed the fruit Paul speaks of in Romans. Her testimony is a living picture of the perseverance and hope that rises when we choose to look toward God during those seasons of hardship, even when we have no idea how we're going to move forward or how God is going to get us through unforeseen pain.

She's an unexpected widow and mother to seven children, and she'll be the first to tell you the former title is one she never wanted or thought would be part of her future.

In the early, dark hours of the morning eight years ago, Lisa was awoken abruptly by her husband Dan's labored breathing. At first, she thought he was having a nightmare and tried to console him back to sleep. However, upon further examination, she realized something was terribly wrong. Her husband wasn't dreaming. He was struggling for air.

After turning on the lights and seeing her husband's face, Lisa knew she needed to call 911. The person on the other end of the line walked her through CPR as her son made sure her younger kids went upstairs, away from the alarming scene. Every time she stopped to take Dan's pulse, she was unable to find one, and her mind went back and forth between the reality of the situation and hope that he would somehow pull through. Once the paramedics arrived, they ushered Lisa out of the room as they administered medicine and tried to revive him.

Her sister and close friends were already at the hospital when Lisa arrived after following the ambulance there. She remembers it was eerily quiet. She expected chaos and rushing around, but there was none. What she soon discovered was that the paramedics were never able to resuscitate her husband. Her forty-eight-year-old high school sweetheart with whom she had just vacationed was gone. He had seemed perfectly healthy, and there were no indications anything was wrong with him. Now, she was going to have to find the words to tell her seven kids that they no longer had a father. She recalls one of her teenage sons waiting for her in the driveway when she arrived home from the emergency room, anxious for an update after several phone calls to his mom.

Although it's a normal reaction for people to question God when they experience grief, especially of this magnitude, Lisa never became angry with him or asked why. But she says there were many occasions when she asked, "What now?" How was she going to raise these kids without a father figure in their lives? How were her boys going to become men without their dad to guide them and help equip them the way dads were intended to do? After Dan's funeral, Lisa remembers going to a trail she frequented often and speaking to God out loud. Her cry was earnest and straightforward. She said if she was going to get through this, he was going to have to be like the pillar of fire and cloud, just as he was for the Israelites.

While she didn't hear an audible voice, his Spirit spoke firmly and told her if she would stay in his Word, he would give her exactly what she needed to get through each day. Lisa obeyed, and God kept his promise. Early each morning before the kids got up, she would open her Bible, not even knowing what that day's reading would hold. And every day, there was a treasure. A nugget planted within the pages specifically for that day, delivering enough hope for her to put one foot in front of the other until bedtime. She claimed God's promise to be a Defender of the widow and a Father to the fatherless. She took him at his word and believed him, and her faith sustained her.

Lisa's reliance on God and his Word through her suffering produced the perseverance Paul talks about in Romans 5:3–5. It was a decision to keep seeking, day in and day out. And through this daily resolve, he molded her character. You see, suffering often causes us to react in two ways. We either yield or harden.

Yielding to His Hand

Have you ever watched someone blow glass? It is a breathtaking experience to watch something we know as hard, resilient, and strong as metal become bendable and pliant to touch. When the glassblower pulls the blowpipe out of the furnace, the glass on the end of it glows bright orange, as if indicating its readiness to be made into something magnificent. What makes the glass responsive to the oxygen released into it and the touch of the artist's hand is the temperature. Without putting the material into heat that often exceeds two thousand degrees, the blower would never be able to craft it into anything other than a shapeless blob. It's simply too stiff and resistant. In the same way that molten glass becomes viscous enough to shape and blow air into when it's pulled out of fiery heat, sorrow and pain can make us more responsive to God's touch. We become more reactive and receptive to his hand. But the key is letting him shape us instead of resisting it.

When the piece of art is finished being shaped and transformed, it is placed in an annealer where it is cooled at a controlled rate. Not using this other type of furnace could result in thermal shock, making the glass unusable. By cooling the artwork at a steady, managed temperature, the blowers ensure the glass will keep its rigid molecular structure, making it strong and solid. But the attentiveness that the glassblower uses in doing this doesn't compare to the care God uses with each one of us when we're going through the fire. Our pain does not go unnoticed by him, and he is aware of each tear that falls, each prayer sent, and every day we don't want to get out of bed because of the grief consuming us.

After Dan's death, during situations when Lisa would normally go to her husband for wisdom and advice, she had to turn to God and lean on him with everything she had. There were many nights she cried herself to sleep, not knowing how she was going to make it alone, having to learn the parenting curve all over again as a single mom. But she kept going to God. He became that pillar of fire she needed and her guide in ways she'd never experienced before.

Lisa says she would never want the tragedy she's experienced for anyone. But she also says she'd never want to go back to the woman she was before Dan's death.

"In our heartbreak and in our hardest hard, God reshapes our heart to look like his," Lisa says.[1] Even though Dan's absence is still felt eight years later and the big events like graduations and weddings contain a gap no one can fill, Lisa has seen the presence of God each day. She's seen him give her words and strength when she didn't think she had anything left to give. She's seen him through friends showing up at her doorstep when she didn't even know she'd need them. Now she has a son who has landed a competitive residency in the Air Force and a daughter who is doing medical missions in Brazil. She's a grandmother, and God has poured blessing upon blessing into her life. But the joy is still mixed with grief and mourning an absence that will forever be felt. The blessings are blended with a heartache that sometimes surfaces out of nowhere.

Would Lisa have experienced the perseverance that produces character, and character, hope without the suffering? Couldn't there have been another way? I don't think we'll ever know the answer to this question while we're on this side of eternity. But as I hear this woman of God and friend tell her story, I see that those words in Romans aren't empty platitudes or wishful thinking. They're true. She is living proof of it.

> Suffering trains our eyes to see God in places we've never noticed him, because when we suffer we become more like him than ever before.

Suffering trains our eyes to see God in places we've never noticed him, because when we suffer we become more like him than ever before. Just like Jesus cried out to the Father in the Garden of Gethsemane as he faced torture, unthinkable pain, and death, we cry out to him for our next breath. We yearn for him and search for him in each and every detail of our lives, because without him we can't survive. Lisa will be the first to tell you that during those first months after Dan's death, she saw God in places she'd never even thought to look because she needed to see evidence of God's presence to survive. She needed to know he was there to continue placing one foot in front of the other.

Do we look for him when everything is going well and everyone is happy? Sometimes. But during the seasons when we're not sure how we'll get through the day, we cling to him like a drowning person longs for air. It's how we're designed. A look at some of the words David penned during times of hardship shows how desperate we become for God's presence when his presence is all we have.

As the deer pants for streams of water,
so my soul pants for you, my God. (Ps. 42:1)

David goes on to say his tears have been his food day and night (Ps. 42:3). He didn't write these words when everything in his life was perfect and trouble-free. He wrote them with urgency. He needed God to intervene. If you've ever seen a deer run through a dense forest toward a stream of fresh water, you get a sense of the distressed nature of David's words.

While we need God each and every moment, even when life is good, suffering has a way of magnifying a crucial facet of our human nature: that without God, we are incomplete. When we're soaring on the tails of an incredible experience like a wedding or a birth, we don't always feel it. But when we're in the depths of a darkness, we know it with every ounce of our being.

This is why we rejoice. This is why we continue worshipping the God who walks alongside us through it. Because we get to experience him in a way many people never do. Because we get to see him in places we never thought we'd find him.

Becoming the Proof

We are one of the key ways God shows himself during those periods when life falls apart. When I received my husband's text about his dad, all I wanted to do was hug him and be present. He was working at the time, and the space between us seemed to grow wider with each passing minute. Prayer became my embrace. My pleas to our Father became my comfort until he came home later that evening.

This is the other reason suffering can be a gift: because when we walk through it, God's people come together in a way where his presence is palpable. Other's feet at our threshold are his feet walking through our door. A friend's arms wrapped around us are his strong grasp letting us know we don't have to move forward alone.

The day after our twelve-year anniversary, we waited for a delayed surgery. Hours inched by at a pace slow enough to hear the seconds ticking. My husband and brother-in-law sat in the hospital while I stayed at home with the kids, responding to messages and reaching out to as many praying sisters as I could. Sometimes waiting can be the worst torture of all. Our minds become their own combat zone as we continually fight against the lies of the enemy. Lies that try to predict the outcome. Lies saying God has forsaken us or telling us this situation is a result of God's punishment. These moments are when we need other followers of Jesus speaking the truth over us. We need brothers and sisters to raise our hands like Aaron and Hur held Moses's hands during the battle against the Amalekites (Exod. 17). This unity and refusal to let someone grapple through the darkness alone is how we see God. It's how others who are watching and may have never witnessed his power and grace will see him too.

Seeing God doesn't always mean we get what we want. My friend Lisa cried out to God for mercy when the paramedics were working on her husband, and she'll be the first to tell you the outcome was not what she wanted. But God still showed mercy. He showed mercy through the friends who showed up at the hospital, and he continues to show it eight years later as her children thrive despite not having their father with them.

As we prayed over my father-in-law and anticipated what would come next, I saw his mercy too. He showed his compassion and attentiveness through friends and family who prayed across the globe. Many of them had never met Chris's dad, and probably never will. But when one sister or brother reaches out to another, the ties of blood and relationship don't matter. We are all one because of his body, and hardship has a way of connecting us like nothing else does.

At one point in the evening, the kids were getting louder and louder as I tried to get them to bed, and I could feel my blood pressure rising as I thought to myself, "This is taking too long. What is going on?" I immediately prayed again, asking for God's protection. And less than a half hour later, I received the text. The surgery was successful. Everything went as expected and, barring any unforeseen complications, he would be released the next day.

Would God have still been present if the outcome had been different? Would he still be faithful? These are difficult questions to think about, but they need to be asked. And while we won't dwell on the what-ifs or the unknowns, the answer is yes.

> Hardship causes us to see God's presence as a gift rather than an entitlement.

Hardship causes us to see God's presence as a gift rather than an entitlement. So often, we take his presence for granted. We can come to him any time and anywhere, whether we just talked to him yesterday or it's been years since we've made conversation with him a priority. And this is what he wants us to do. He desires our devotion and relationship. But he also wants us to realize who he is. Holy. Set apart. Worthy of our worship no matter what is taking place in our lives.

There are still many answers about my father-in-law's health we don't yet have. And as we come to God, he shows up in the wait. We draw to him through the daily decision to focus our minds on him instead of the uncertainty. Although there's no exact blueprint for how to fix your mind on him, there are some actions we can take.

1. **Instead of asking why, ask God to show you the next step.** I love how my friend Lisa chose to ask God, "Now what?" instead of why. It's a question he can answer. Even if God were to answer the why, we probably wouldn't understand because we are still living in fallen, mortal bodies. As it states in Isaiah, his thoughts are higher than our thoughts and his ways higher than our ways (Isa. 55:9). But if we ask him to give us a next step, he can direct us. We're given a course of action instead of demanding what we think we deserve.

2. **Worship instead of worry.** When we praise God despite our circumstances, something amazing happens. He changes us. Even though our situation may remain the same, we see it with a different set of eyes and we worry less. Instead of being consumed by a thousand questions and unknowns, we're consumed by his peace and comfort. We see God is sovereign over it, even if we don't see a way out.

3. **Extend hands to others and ask for help.** Often, our initial reaction when trouble hits is to isolate ourselves or focus inward. We become anxious and try to carry the

weight all by ourselves instead of reaching out to others. This is exactly what the enemy wants us to do. He wants us to feel isolated and alone. But when we let others assist us in our time of need, we're not only allowing them to bless us, but allowing the helper to be blessed too. The benefits are manifold, and this is God's design. It's also one of the ways he makes himself visible during seasons when it's often difficult to see his hand.

While we may never usher in suffering like a welcome guest, our perspective on it can make a life-changing difference. And when we walk through it, we can know for certain God's feelings toward us haven't changed. He still pursues us with a love that endured the worst agony imaginable to be with us. So instead of questioning the presence of his love, let's walk in it with confidence. Let's claim freedom from doubt because of our certainty in who he is.

Adjusting Our Lens

1. Is there an area of your life where God may want to do work through your pain? Do you see the work he's doing as valuable, even though he hasn't taken away the pain and suffering?
2. Have you ever experienced a season that, like Lisa, you wouldn't wish on anyone, but after going through it you were changed for the better? How did God transform you through it?

6

The Power of Perspective

Before giving birth to my firstborn over ten years ago, I thought "mom brain" was a myth. In my mind, it was an excuse to completely forget plans you made weeks ago because they became inconvenient. A reason to blow off that person you really didn't want to have lunch with anyway, because you'd rather not hit them with honesty.

Then motherhood arrived with all of its sleepless nights and 3 a.m. diaper changes, and I realized: I was wrong. Yesterday, when my son came home with a reminder about the Fall Fun Night that I was supposed to buy juice boxes for, it hit me again with full force. It is real. It's an epidemic. And it makes me grateful for modern technology where you can schedule those little reminders on your phone. Unfortunately, I don't always remember to do those either.

As much as I would like to blame every instance of forgetfulness on being a mom, I realize it's not a motherhood condition as much as it is a human condition. Especially when it comes to faith.

One look at the Bible is evidence of this state of spiritual amnesia. We need continual reminders not only of who God is, but who we are as a result. We need the truth to be repeated over and over. Why? Because we live in a world where lies and half-truths are constant and loud.

The recurring theme and story of the Bible isn't one of people who are self-sufficient and able to find truth on their own. It is one of people rejecting God's truth, looking to other sources for fulfillment, and God drawing them back to himself.

But there's good news too. In nearly every account of individuals going astray, there's one faithful servant who refuses to be deceived. There's one person who holds fast to God's Word. Although they're far from perfect, God uses these women and men because he sees what's in their hearts.

So what makes them different? How are these common people with problems just like everyone else able to stand firm and see God's truth when everyone else is misled? Although there are many reasons, there's one habit we see over and over again. They build altars. In a world where people believe truth is fluid, followers of God build altars to remind them it's unchanging.

> In a world where people believe truth
> is fluid, followers of God build altars
> to remind them it's unchanging.

We see this practice occur whenever God gives his men and women victory over an obstacle that seems insurmountable or he reveals a new truth about himself. Their actions show an awareness of their propensity to forget, so instead of allowing themselves to, they are proactive in making sure they remember. Instead of trusting their own memory, which is frequently shown to be short, they build pillars of truth. Each stone is a mental note and praise to the faithful One who brought them there.

Often, men and women of Scripture don't stop there. They give the Lord a new name reflecting the unique way he has revealed his love for them during the struggle they just survived. We see this type of worship in Exodus after Israel defeats the Amalekites, who had tormented and attacked Israel for years. Moses recalls the way his people were able to gain victory over their enemy: while his hands were raised. As long as Moses's hands were in the air, Israel won. When Moses became tired, Aaron and Hur stepped in to support their leader by holding his hands up.

God doesn't simply give Israel a short-term victory. He completely wipes out the Amalekites' name. Moses knows how significant this moment is. He realizes what God has done and wants to remember his steadfast love. Because of his great delivery from the hands of their enemy, Moses takes action:

> Moses built an altar and called it The LORD is my
> Banner. He said, "Because hands were lifted up against
> the throne of the LORD, the LORD will be at war
> against the Amalekites from generation to generation."
> (Exod. 17:15–16)

Instead of moving on to the next task or job, Moses stops. He takes stock of what God has done. He creates not only a visual reminder, but also an audible statement of truth, "The LORD is my Banner," so that he and the entire nation of Israel won't forget. He doesn't let the forward-moving momentum his people have gained from such a sizeable victory keep him from pausing, worshipping, and building.

So how can we apply this practice to our own lives and remember God's faithfulness when things spin out of control? One of the best ways to remember is to identify the times when we forget. To ask ourselves what areas make us question God and lose sight of each time he's delivered us in the past.

I will never ask my readers to do anything I'm not willing to do myself, and I asked myself the same question you're asking yourself right now. God has a way of pinpointing those areas of our lives where we'd rather brush aside our fears, insecurities, and doubts and pretend they're not there. When I thought over each detail of my days and was truly honest with myself and with him, one love came to mind: my kids.

Facing Our Fear to Remember His Truth

The first time my firstborn had an allergic reaction to food, he was a year old. I had no clue what was going on, but I knew something was seriously wrong. My husband and I were settling into our bedtime routine, and we pulled off Jaden's shirt to bathe him. Hives covered his body and his face was visibly swelling more with each passing second. Thank God my husband had experience with allergies and immediately knew how severe the outcome could be. Within a couple of minutes, we were in the car, racing toward the urgent care place down the road.

My husband drove eighty in a forty-mile-per-hour zone while I listened to Jaden's breathing, which was becoming more labored the further we drove. Upon arrival at the urgent care place, they told us they were not equipped to handle allergic reactions. I wanted to yell at the lady standing behind the counter, asking her if she could see that my son needed medical attention, but we didn't have time to waste.

Instead, we sped to the hospital, where we were immediately taken back to the triage nurse. They administered an antihistamine injection and monitored him while the swelling went down, and his breathing returned to normal. The staff repeatedly told us we were lucky. They told us it could have been much worse. But we knew luck didn't have anything to do with it. God was there the whole time, even when I was in a state of panic that made it difficult to move or think. He got us to that hospital on time, and he made sure we didn't get pulled over when my husband flew at light speed down Harrison Boulevard. Instead of getting a police escort, we had an escort by the Protector.

Even as I write those words, I know there are others who are grieving babes who took that final breath in the hospital or on the way there. There are others who never had the opportunity to meet their child face to face and hold him or her in their arms. I wish I could hug you and sit with you over a cup of coffee, but I want you to know this: God sees your pain. Your grief is not pushed aside or swept under the rug, but understood by the One who feels every depth of pain we feel.

My son survived, but I know many have entered heaven's gates far too soon. I don't want to pretend everything always turns out the way we hoped, but I do want to talk about how our fears can make us forget God's faithfulness. Because after the first incident (and yes, there were others) with my son, I had to face a very real fear: the fear that God would take my child.

After my son's initial reaction, we discovered he was allergic to tree nuts and peanuts, along with a few other things. We saw an allergist, did a skin-pricking test, and the doctor told us an EpiPen was a must. He gave us a list of things to do and not to do, and with necessary precautions, everything was fine. And I was fine too. Until my son started school.

I remember the first time I received a phone call with the school's number showing on the caller ID. My heartbeat and blood pressure rose faster than I could push the button and say hello.

And no, I'm not exaggerating. Even though it was the nurse calling to make sure my son did *not* consume something he wasn't supposed to eat, I was constantly worried that he would. Anxiety over what might happen consumed me, and I didn't know how to make it stop.

When you're child's life is at stake, you're proactive. You do everything you can to make sure the worst doesn't happen; and I would never suggest that surrendering our fears to God means being irresponsible. I believe God entrusts our kids to us as a gift, and our role as a parent is one of the most important ones given to us. But by constantly worrying and trying to predict what would happen, I was driving myself crazy. And in order to finally let go, I had to look back.

> Sometimes our faith walk requires us to stop looking ahead into the unknown and to instead look back at everything God has done.

Sometimes our faith walk requires us to stop looking ahead into the unknown and to instead look back at everything God has done. Looking back, I saw how he'd protected our son. I saw how in each incident, he'd made sure we arrived at the hospital safely and that our son received the care he needed. I saw how he gave our firstborn an understanding of the severity of his allergy and made his knowledge our first line of defense against possible exposure.

By shifting my focus to God's faithfulness in the past instead of my worry about the future, I was able to let go. At first it was just a little bit. And then a little bit more. Until one day, I made it through a day without anxiety about what might happen. This is what those altars of remembrance can do.

So what if we built one? Not just in our minds, which we've already said are forgetful, but like a modern-day Moses. Then, we would have a physical reminder to help us against spiritual amnesia.

How to Build an Altar of Remembrance

1. Find a clear mason jar or bowl. It doesn't have to be fancy.
2. Buy some light-colored stones at your local craft store; or if you live in an area where stones are prevalent, find some around your home.
3. Each time God answers a prayer, provides a need, or clears a path, record it by writing on one of your stones with a Sharpie or maker. It can be a one-word testimony: Provider, Deliverer, Comforter.
4. Put your stones in the jar. Each time you need a reminder of God's steadfast character, look at your altar.

Looking Back before We Look Forward

If we look at some well-known heroes in Scripture, we see a similar pattern. We see a decision to look at God's track record of deliverance and fulfillment of his promises more than the uncertainty that lies ahead. One of my favorite examples of this shift in perspective is Rahab. All logic would say this woman had no reason to believe God would do anything to save her, but our God loves using the least likely people to exhibit courage and the transforming power of belief in something greater than ourselves.

Rahab is a prostitute who is introduced when Israel is taking over the Promised Land they waited forty years to inherit. Joshua sends two spies into Jericho to survey the region, and they spend the night at her home. When their identity is discovered, it seems her gut reaction should be to hand them over to the authorities. After all, she isn't an Israelite. She isn't part of God's chosen people. But instead, she helps them. She hides them on the roof and resolves not to tell the search party their whereabouts.

Most women in Rahab's situation would look only at the risk and the potential for disaster. Most would worry about being caught and decide the gamble was too great. But rather than look forward at the possible threat, Rahab looks back. She recalls how God faithfully delivered the Israelites in battle and how his power has enabled them to accomplish what appeared to be unattainable.

> I know that the LORD has given you this land and that a great fear of you has fallen on us, so that all who live in this country are melting in fear because of you. We have heard how the LORD dried up the water of the Red Sea for you when you came out of Egypt, and what you did to Sihon and Og, the two kings of the Amorites east of the Jordan, whom you completely destroyed. When we heard of it, our hearts melted in fear and everyone's courage failed because of you, for the LORD your God is God in heaven above and on the earth below. (Josh. 2:9–11)

What blows me away is that this woman isn't recounting things God has done for her or even her family. She's telling of his faithfulness to a nation who is trying to take over her land. And yet, what he's done for others propels her forward, even if it means putting her life in danger.

Rahab's people may have lost their "courage and will to fight," but she hasn't. She's amped up and ready, inspired with bravery and confidence in a God she's seen carry Israel through famine, exile, and battles that seemed impossible to win. She tells the spies if their army will spare her family, she will keep their identity a secret and help them escape. The men agree, and instruct her to tie a scarlet cord in the window when they besiege the city. By doing so, she and her family will be spared.

Not only are Rahab and her family spared, but they become part of God's chosen people. Later in Joshua we're told, "because she hid the men Joshua had sent as spies to Jericho—and she lives among the Israelites to this day" (Josh. 6:25). This woman who was from a completely different culture, had no experience with God or faith, and had lived a life of prostitution changed the course of history and was grafted into God's family.

She remembered all God had done for his people and everything he'd brought them through and said, "I want a Savior like that. I want to be part of something bigger than me." And God honored her. He saw her heart that desired change.

But he didn't stop with his protection of her family or their adoption into his. He wanted to make an even bolder statement. He not only redeemed her past but also exalted her future. When she made her declaration of faith, he'd already written her name in a place where it would never be forgotten: in the lineage of Jesus Christ (Matt. 1:5). Can you think of an affirmation more powerful?

Rahab looked back at the steadfast love God had shown the Israelites and decided he was worth the risk. And this is exactly what we have to do when we're faced with an unknown future. When our fears threaten to derail our faith and make us forget what God has done, we have to take time to stop and remember.

> When our fears threaten to derail our faith and make us forget what God has done, we have to take time to stop and remember.

We remember the times he's shown up, even when we didn't think deliverance from our situation was possible. We recall the way he rescued us from the pit when our darkness seemed too impenetrable for him to shine his light through. This perspective is what will enable us to keep trusting and believing God is there when our feelings tell us otherwise. When difficulty rises, we can stand firm.

Time Brings Perspective

Sometimes we need time and space from a difficult period to see that God's light was shining the whole time. When we're in the middle of it, we're often only focused on the end goal. We may have sensed God calling us to do something, but feel as though we hit a wall. We want breakthrough and deliverance, but God wants us to desire him instead of only desiring to be rescued.

My friend Betsy knows how our tendency to concentrate only on our end objective can keep us from seeing what God is already doing. For many years, her family served as missionaries in a Middle Eastern country where the gospel message is unpopular. The area is predominantly Muslim, and some residents have even been imprisoned for sharing their Christian faith. When she and her husband first arrived there, they faced constant doubt and uncertainty about whether or not they were doing the right thing.

There were many Sundays when they were first starting out that their church had only had nine people in attendance, including children. Betsy recalls how they would sit there and stare at each other, wondering if anyone else they'd invited would come. For months, she was often depressed and discouraged with the slow growth of their ministry; until one day, she realized something. Rather than focus only on their goal of church attendance and growth, she had to remain focused on God. She had to keep taking the next step he'd asked her to take and trust he would move in his time. It was up to him to do the rest.

What gave Betsy this revelation? Time. Years spent doing exactly what God asked her and her family to do. Often, God needs time to work in our hearts to make us see what he sees. As we're working and doing what he's asked, he's cultivating a heart that's able to discern his presence more clearly. He's using what we see as a lack of fruit to purify our motives and make us desire him rather than a specific outcome we think we need to be successful.

In the Sermon on the Mount, Jesus devotes much of his message to talking about who will inherit his kingdom, be honored by God, and see him. He separates those who merely want to look upright from those who actually thirst for it. He separates those who talk about righteousness from those who actually seek it.

In Matthew 5:8 he says, "Blessed are the pure in heart, for they will see God." He doesn't say they might or they may see God. He says they will. But a pure heart isn't something that happens as a result of starting a church or ministry. It isn't a fast track request where we can ask for it and receive it immediately. It's a continual process. It takes time and experiences that God uses to teach us the value of each and every moment spent loving those he loves.

As Betsy and her family broke new ground in the Middle East and shared the gospel in a place desperate for truth, God was purifying their hearts. She looks back now on those first few years of their church planting, and she sees God's hand in the details. She sees how he gave her a go-to friend to whom she could pour her heart out when things were difficult to help keep her sane. She understands how God used those small beginnings to prepare them and cultivate hearts that were ready to pour into others who were thirsty and seeking.

Betsy says, "God did more *in* us than He did *through* us. We learned perseverance, and we learned how to keep God at the center of our God-sized dream."[1]

Betsy not only gained personal perspective from her family's years in ministry, but she's writing about it so others can reap the benefits also. When I hear her share pieces of her story and read about it online, it's not just a beautiful testimony I see, although it is that. I see the unchanging care and attentiveness of a God who never stops moving and showing himself through miracles, even when we don't see them. Even when we doubt and are uncertain that he's there, he's working in ways it may take us years or even a lifetime to see.

The church they planted eventually grew to thirty people. In America where megachurches are in most major cities and we have the ability to attend many on our digital devices, this may not seem like a big deal. But in a Middle Eastern country where few people have any interest in Jesus, it's a miracle. It's a legacy that will live on in a country where two people said "yes" to God, even in the face of unpredictable circumstances.

Leaving a Trail

Each time we say "yes" to God, we leave a trail. We leave a path for others to follow and a legacy of faithfulness for them to cling to when the view ahead is unclear. This is what the women and men of the Bible did for us, and it's what we can do for others when we stop and commemorate those moments of victory.

Remember all the treks up Mount Pisgah with my family? The reason why we were able to reach the summit each time, without fail, is because someone left a track for us to follow. They left visible evidence of their journey through the forest, giving those who came after them confidence that they would be successful too.

When Moses built the altar commemorating their victory over the Amalekites, he created a trail. When Rahab risked her life with no indication of hesitancy or doubt, she left a trail.

You and I can leave a trail too. But first we must pause. We must recognize what God has done and create a tribute to his unwavering character. This act of conviction is what will keep us moving toward the peak when everything around us screams to take a detour. It's what will keep our brothers and sisters united with us when they're unsure of the way.

Adjusting Our Lens

1. Is your natural tendency to pause and celebrate the faith victories in your life or to rush ahead to the next task? How do you think taking time to remember the victories would impact your journey?

2. Is there a person in your life or a hero whose legacy has inspired your spiritual walk? How have the highlights they've shared or recorded helped you continue to pursue God, even when the path didn't look the way you envisioned?

7

His Glory in the Grind

I stood over the laundry pile, which seemed to have gotten bigger in the past five minutes. Was that even possible? Wishing the clothes would sort themselves, I pulled them out of the hamper and began separating, hoping to finish the task and work on an article before my daughter woke from her nap. But as I got through folding the load and putting it away, I heard her cry. I let out an audible sigh and waited a few minutes, hoping she would quiet and go back to sleep. She didn't.

Her cries turned to jabber as I opened her door, giving her my best, tired mama smile. She grinned as she pulled herself up and bounced with delight, pointing to the rocker. After changing her diaper, I sat down and granted her request, nursing her while we rocked. Writing inspiration came and, trying to seize the moment, I typed a few paragraphs using the notes app on my phone. But before I could come to a satisfying stopping point, Elise became squirmy and I had to put the phone back on the dresser.

When afternoon arrived and we rode down to the bus stop to pick up the boys, I fought against that old, familiar thought creeping into the recesses of my mind: I didn't get anything done today. It was a feeling I was well acquainted with. It first reared its head nearly ten years before when I left my full-time office job. And even though I loathed the job I walked away from, it boasted a few advantages that being a stay-at-home mom never did. The main one? Measurable progress that was recognized. When I was doing well, I knew it, and my boss affirmed it.

My job was a collector for high-risk auto loans. It wasn't exactly a dream career, but it helped pay the bills and was a huge answer to prayer after our cross-country move. Although the job was high stress and at times very demanding, I knew where I stood when it came to results and numbers. The lower the amount in our delinquent queue, the happier my supervisor was. And my schedule? It was the same every day, with the exception of overtime.

When I came home after delivering our first child, I felt like I had no compass. Not only were we thousands of miles from any family, but I was isolated from anyone except my baby. There wasn't a checklist to tell me if I was mothering well. There was no schedule. No one saw any of the work I did on a day-to-day basis, so it was almost as though it didn't exist. There were days it seemed as though I was becoming one with the walls in our three-bedroom rancher.

Isn't it interesting how we equate what is seen with what is valuable? Even though I know in my core that my role as a mother was exponentially more important than my position as a collector, there were days I questioned whether or not it mattered. Not because I didn't love my child, but because I didn't think anyone noticed. There is a place in each of our souls that longs for significance, but until we recognize the One who truly sees us, we will spend our lives lost and wandering.

> There is a place in each of our souls
> that longs for significance, but until we
> recognize the One who truly sees us, we
> will spend our lives lost and wandering.

One morning in early fall, I sat at a MOPS meeting craving connection with other living, breathing adults. Hoping to meet just one person who would not throw things on the floor, expecting me to pick them up. I listened to the coordinator announce the year's theme, and then relaxed into my chair as she dimmed the lights and played a video.

Images of moms caring for their babes flickered across the screen. Some were rocking infants and others were pushing toddlers in swings, but they all shared a common bond. They were mothers. And even though the images were beautiful, it was the words read throughout the scenes that pierced my soul in the best possible way. A woman was reciting Psalm 139. Even though I'd gone to a Christian high school and studied this psalm several times before, it was as though I was hearing it for the first time.

A place deep inside that God had been trying to reach unlocked, and tears flowed down my cheeks. I took deep breaths and tried to regain my composure, but as a looked around, I realized others were crying too.

You have searched me, LORD,
and you know me.
You know when I sit and when I rise;
you perceive my thoughts from afar.

You discern my going out and my lying down;
you are familiar with all my ways. (Ps. 139:1–3)

Hearing those words David penned years ago, I realized God not only saw me; he treasured me. He saw places I didn't dare to reveal to anyone. Places that longed for acknowledgment, meaning, and purpose. Places where I questioned my worth and wanted someone to simply pat me on the back and tell me I was doing okay. The truth was, I felt selfish and even silly for wanting those things. But God saw my need and the desire of my heart, and in a room filled with other moms who I'm sure were feeling the same needs, he cared about me specifically. He spoke to me in a way I could understand.

In that instant, I finally understood how sacred the work I did in the home was. Both to my family and to God. It didn't matter how many people saw it. It didn't matter if it was just me and my son, and I was covered in pee and poop at 3 a.m. God was right there with us. He was glorified in the tired, unseen, and mundane as much as he was in the victories I shared with others. Perhaps even more so, because those were the moments when I became most like Jesus. Laying down my rights and what I thought I deserved. Laying down myself to serve the needs of someone else.

Yes, these moments honored God. And on a fall morning in a room full of other moms, my eyes were opened. Because of a shift in the way I viewed those weary hours making me a mom, I finally saw a glimpse of what God did.

Leveling the Field

My pastor knows what it means to lay down your rights and the things you think you deserve to serve others, but the lesson didn't come easy for him. There's a story he's told our congregation countless times, but it holds truths we often need to hear. You see, our lead pastor never thought he'd start a church or preach from a pulpit. His passion was, and still is, for kids and teens, and for many years he was the children's pastor at a large church. But before he taught any kids, he drove a bus, and this is the testimony he loves to tell.

One of his early mentors in ministry was Pastor Jim Cymbala of the New Brooklyn Tabernacle church in New York. When Bob first began working there, he was young and green. He was itching for a job. More importantly, he was itching for something that would earn him valuable experience. Something that would put him in front of others, teaching or leading in a realm he considered beneficial. Driving a bus for inner city kids was the last thing he had on his mind, but this is exactly what the church needed.

Since he didn't feel like he could say no, Bob agreed to do it. Although he didn't outwardly complain, he was seething on the inside. He thought the job was beneath him and he should be doing something more worthwhile. He thought he had skills and talents that were being wasted and could be better used elsewhere. At the time, he didn't realize how crucial this responsibility was. He saw it as the lowest possible task on the totem pole of ministry, and he couldn't wait for them to find someone else to step up and fill the role.

One day Bob was on his regular route to pick up the kids and take them to the Bible camp the church hosted every week. He was certain God didn't have anything for him to learn while doing this mundane job, so his mindset was, "Let's hurry up and get this over with." He didn't make much eye contact with anyone; he was just trying to get from point A to point B as quickly as possible. But at one stop, a little girl who came up to his chest as he sat in the driver's seat just stood there and stared at him. She didn't go straight to her seat like the others who were boarding. Sensing that this girl wasn't going anywhere until he acknowledged her,

Bob turned and looked her in the eyes. Although he didn't mutter his thoughts out loud, he kept wondering, "What does she want? Can't she see we need to get going?"

Giving him an immediate answer to his inner monologue, the girl came close and kissed him on the cheek. That was all she wanted. She didn't ask him any questions or desire anything from him. Satisfied, she went and sat down. And Bob Ryan was never the same. Sensing the Holy Spirit's gentle, yet firm conviction, he confessed his bitter attitude and felt the Spirit's presence right there with him. All because of a little girl who saw him, he realized God saw him too. He finally understood that without driving the bus, this girl would never have the opportunity to hear about Jesus. She would never know the message of the gospel and how there was a God who loved her and desired a relationship with her.

Those hundreds of kids who joined their ministry each week were there because someone drove them. And during this particular season, it was Bob Ryan. Each person in the church worked to fill his or her part, and because they came together as a body, lives were transformed. Decisions were made to follow Jesus. One person wasn't any more important than another, because without each one, the entire ministry would suffer.

In Colossians, we see there isn't any differentiation between the seemingly big works and the small. All of it is to bring glory to God: "And whatever you do, whether in word or deed, do it all in the name of the Lord Jesus, giving thanks to God the Father through him" (Col. 3:17). Paul doesn't tell us to only do those things that are visible to others to the glory of Jesus. He doesn't say to make an effort only when we think we're on a huge platform teaching others or when we're doing something we think is making good use of our time and talent. He says to do it *all* to the glory of God. Every word we speak. Every action we perform.

Why? Because to Jesus, all of it is important. Whether we're driving the bus or scrubbing the floors in the bathroom, when we do it because we love him and want others to love him too, it matters.

Eventually, Bob moved from driving the bus to teaching those inner city kids. Later, he became a children's pastor, and now he is the lead pastor at a growing church plant. None of these things happened overnight. But in each season, he was diligent with what God gave him, realizing after a pivotal moment on a bus how critical it was for the members of the body to work together as a light illuminating the One who *is* the Light.

Sometimes, we think those with a microphone or those who stand in front of an audience have more of Jesus than we do. Or perhaps we believe he holds them in higher esteem because of the way they're perceived. But you know what? If you and I were sitting over coffee right now, I'd lean in close and whisper a little secret to you: At the foot of the cross, not one of his children shines any brighter than another. We are all stars because of Christ's light in us.

> At the foot of the cross, not one of his children shines any brighter than another. We are all stars because of Christ's light in us.

The Purpose of Our Light

When we come to know Christ, he gives each of us a lamp. Whether we're aware of it or not, it's there and he intends for us to use it. But there are times when God uses us to illuminate the works of others. Not so people will merely see someone else's works, but so they'll see God. This other person on whom you shine the light may have the exact gifts, experiences, or passions needed to point a wandering soul toward Jesus. Recognition and accolades are never the point. It's all about allowing people to recognize where the light that never fades comes from.

One of my favorite ways to spend quality time with my first-born is to go to the theater. A few years ago, we went to see a live production of Mary Poppins, and the entire event was mesmerizing from start to finish. Although it was tempting to grab my phone and capture some of the production on camera, there was a strict no phone or flash photography rule, so I kept it tucked away in my purse.

While our eyes were fixed on the actors onstage, I was well aware that there was an entire crew behind the scenes of the play, controlling the lighting, sound, cues, and other necessary tasks. Can you imagine if the lighting crew had decided to take the evening off? Or if they had decided their role wasn't important enough or become disillusioned by the fact that they weren't on stage, and had decided to go home? It would've been a complete disaster, and the entire night would have been ruined.

In the same way, God sometimes uses us more behind the scenes than in front of an audience. He may use us to draw someone's attention to another person in a lead role because leadership is his or her gifting. During the season when Pastor Bob drove the bus, God was preparing him and using his lamp to shine toward those who were teachers and leaders in the children's ministry. He may use us in the same way, and ask us to invite someone who loves music and theater to an event where these talents are displayed. This doesn't mean the work we're doing isn't meaningful. It doesn't mean God values us any less than someone who is in the spotlight. As a matter of fact, he may move us into a more prominent position when he knows we're ready. But we'll never be ready if we spend our time sulking and coveting the appointment of someone else. If we want to be a light, we must realize we are working for God even when no one else is looking.

> If we want to be a light, we must realize we are working for God even when no one else is looking.

Ultimately, the end goal of our light is never to illuminate ourselves or even someone else. It's to allow others to experience the Lord. When we shift our focus from, "How can I use this lamp so others see me?" to "How can I point it so others will see him?" something beautiful happens. It's as though a weight is lifted. Because our attention is less on ourselves and more on the Creator, a new sense of purpose emerges. Joy fills us. This type of joy is contagious to others around us and becomes a magnet for those who have yet to taste the Living Water where it's born.

A Change Others Can See

His water nourishes and restores us when we drink of it often. And when we do, others notice. We may not perceive it at first, but they do. Jesus's presence within has a way of changing us in all the best possible ways, and when people look at us, they will wonder what's different.

The first time a friend commented on how my demeanor and attitude had evolved since making the choice to surrender to God's plan for my life, we were driving home from dinner with some other moms. This friend had only known me for a year or so, and when we'd first met, I was eight months pregnant with my firstborn. Anxiousness and fear were my constant companions. We lived over two thousand miles from family, and while attending a party with my husband's work colleagues, one person bluntly asked me, "What are you going to do?" This question did nothing to boost my confidence, and after delivery, my emotions quickly spiraled out of control.

My friend, Adri, was one of the few people other than my husband who saw me both lost in the pit of depression as well as after God lifted me out and placed my feet on firm ground. She was there for all of it, and she witnessed the transformation.

"I see a difference in you just in the short time I've known you," she said. We were driving up a mountain along the Wasatch Front, and the scenery around us seemed to represent the uphill battle I fought for the first eleven months of my son's life.

Further explanation from Adri wasn't needed, but my heart leaped. It was the first time I realized someone saw the change other than me. It wasn't something that was simply taking place inside. It was visible. It was evident to others. Without doing anything other than keeping a friendship with this person who blessed my life in numerous ways, I was sharing the gospel. His presence within was renewing my mind, my perspective, and each aspect of my life, and the renewal was noticeable. First to others; then to me.

> When we allow Jesus to work on us inside,
> the change will be evident on the outside.

When we allow Jesus to work on us inside, the change will be evident on the outside. We will become living testimonies of his grace and goodness. It won't matter if we're in the throes of motherhood, getting up for midnight feedings, or if we're sharing a message on a stage in front of hundreds of women. He will use us no matter what our life looks like or what seemingly tedious job we're doing. The key is surrendering to his plan and his timing. We must allow him to mold us and shape us into vessels who will radiate his light, even when we have no idea how he could possibly use us in our current situation. Even when we would rather be doing something else.

Most of us don't realize others are watching us. They may not comment on what they observe, and sometimes people only remark when they see something negative. But when we make an active choice to live for God, he will use us in the big moments and in those that seem irrelevant.

Living for him looks in the everyday something like this:

- Worshipping him, even when no one else is watching
- Doing each task in our day with excellence, even when it's not something we enjoy
- Acknowledging his hand in the small moments as much as the big ones
- Silencing the noise around us enough to sense his prompting, and then following it

There are hundreds of other things we can do to speak God's love in a language others can understand. But the point is this: be his love letter in every area of your life, and he will use you. We don't need others to commend us or acknowledge us to be his letter. As a matter of fact, many times they won't. When someone praises the energy you pour into living your life well, let him or her know it is a gift from God. Give thanks. Tuck it into your pocket to save for later, when you may be discouraged. And then, keep going.

In 2 Corinthians, Paul tells us:

> You yourselves are our letter, written on our hearts,
> known and read by everyone. You show that you are
> a letter from Christ, the result of our ministry, written
> not with ink but with the Spirit of the living God, not
> on tablets of stone but on tablets of human hearts.
> (2 Cor. 3:2–3)

Can we camp on these words and let them transform our thoughts for a moment? The Spirit of the Living God is writing a letter on our hearts. And through each of these unique letters, he's also writing to the individuals we come into contact with each day. His message isn't read by only a select few; as Paul says, it is "read by everyone."

To the cranky, teething toddler who won't be consoled, you are a letter. To the widowed neighbor next door, you are a letter. To the crazy coupon lady in front of you in the checkout line at the market, you are a letter.

These people matter. They matter to God, and we may be the only connection with him that they have in their day-to-day lives. Are we leaving them with a glimpse of his love or with a bitter taste in their mouths? Are we taking as much care with these ordinary, seemingly insignificant interactions as we do with the mountaintop moments or the ones on a stage? Because when we do, God sees.

As he sees us guarding these connections and knowing they are an opportunity from him, he honors us with more. He may move us into an area of greater visibility where his light can shine even brighter for all to witness. But first we have to acknowledge what we have. First, we have to recognize all of it is grace.

Adjusting Our Lens

1. Let's take a deeper look at Colossians 3:23 and examine the areas of our lives we often overlook. List some examples of day-to-day activities you don't think of as bringing glory to God or as being part of your calling. Then, commit to worshipping God through those things whether by change in attitude, prayer, or simply talking to him while doing them.

2. Have you ever received praise for something you did well when you didn't think anyone was paying attention? How did it make you feel? Think of some ways you can pay closer attention to those people in your life who may be flying under the radar, and ways you can encourage them.

8

A Legalistic Lens or a Grace-Filled Heart?

For much of my life, I approached God through the lens of legalism. In my view, a good God would follow a certain set of rules formulated by me, his imperfect creation. And although I wasn't aware I projected this distorted way of thinking into our relationship, it became clear during the six months we lived in my in-laws' basement.

One overcast, grey afternoon in February, I sat with our two-year-old son, trying to find the right words to pray. I wanted to have faith that things were going to work out and remember God's deliverance in the past, but my resolve was dwindling. Our house sat over two thousand miles away on the other side of the country, unsellable.

I watched our toddler play with his trucks, carefree and without worry. His home was wherever we were, and Momma and

Dada were his safety net. As he made engine noises and used the futon as a racetrack, I secretly wished I could be a kid again. The piles of bills, stresses, and responsibilities felt like weights crushing me, and I struggled to catch my breath. My shoulders were tight with the tension of the prior few weeks.

Our little family moved two months earlier to pursue a job opportunity for my husband. After living in northern Utah for over four years and building a life there, we didn't take the decision lightly. The Wasatch front was our community, and the church where we actively served was our family. We'd grown to love the town where we welcomed our first child, the mountains, and even the winter snow. My husband and I learned to ski together and often hiked the trails surrounding our neighborhood. This place wasn't just a bucket list stop on a map of places to live. It was our home.

We spent much time in prayer, consulting with other believers and seeking God's guidance. We felt sure we had received a green light to move forward. But then one disaster after another followed. With each bump in the road, I questioned our decision.

When we realized our house would not be sellable without taking a huge financial hit, we decided to rent it. We waited months trying to find the right family to move in, and since we couldn't take on two mortgages, our plans to find a new home were put on hold. For months, my husband commuted eighty miles each way from his parents' house to get to work. Each day, he grew a little wearier.

One day he walked into the house after I'd had a huge argument with his mother, and I simply said, "Let's get outta here."

We sat at the local Mexican restaurant eating chips and queso, barely able to say a word to each other. The dark circles under our eyes and heavy slowness of our movement spoke the words we were unable to say to each other.

Talking to God felt the same way. Often, I wondered if he even heard the prayers I offered. Were they making any difference? Did he see how this season was affecting our marriage? Our family? I wasn't sure how long we could continue this way. It felt like we were in a permanent state of limbo, and there was no indication of when it would end.

Although I didn't admit it out loud, I felt slighted by God. The prayers I prayed during the first month after we moved turned robotic and weak. Since he was not answering the way I thought he would, I didn't know what to say. Should I just continue asking for the same thing over and over?

"If he is God, he will answer this way." This was the approach I was taking with the Lord. Although I wasn't fully aware of it, I see it now.

I thought God's love for me was dependent on him responding to my prayers the way I wanted. And while God loves us more than we can imagine, our relationship with him is so much more than this. Sometimes a response is delayed because God wants us to shift our perspective from what we want to what we need. And what I needed was to see God for who he truly was—a Father. Not a distant deity but someone who wanted to be part of every aspect of my life.

Relationship over Legalism

Throughout my middle and high school years, I went to a private Christian academy. Scripture memorization, Bible study, and old hymns were a part of my daily and weekly routines. I knew the Word because I was required to know it. I followed a strict disciplinary code because if I didn't, consequences such as suspension and even expulsion would result. Before I started attending there, the staff required me to read their rulebook and sign my name, showing my willingness to behave according to the school's standards.

This meant no secular concerts, no dances, no smoking cigarettes or consuming alcohol. No relations with your boyfriend, on or off campus. The list went on and on, and for several years, I followed it to a tee. I was the good girl, and I prided myself on it.

But eventually, I grew tired. Actually, I wasn't just tired. I was angry. I looked at the hypocritical lifestyle of some of my fellow classmates, teachers, and church members and wondered why I needed to adhere to the rules when they didn't. I questioned why God seemed to bless these people while I struggled to fit in with the popular crowd and cliques.

In the end, it was the legalistic lens through which I viewed Christianity that pushed me away from God and the church. My senior year, I went further and further down a path of self-destructive, poor choices until, after numerous suspensions, I was expelled from school. Although my grades enabled me to graduate with the rest of my class, I spent the last two weeks of my senior year at home, panicked about my uncertain future.

As I walked out to my car on the day of my expulsion with tears streaming down my face, one of my classmates ran outside to tell me goodbye. His face was full of compassion and genuine concern. He asked me what happened and listened while I told him bits and pieces of the news. I was still in a state of shock, and my words came out jumbled. But I could tell he wasn't trying to get information to start gossip or rumors. He wanted to lend a listening ear.

"Keep your chin up, girl," he said before patting me on the shoulder and turning to walk back inside.

I nodded and tried to muster up a smile. Although I couldn't see it at the time, his interaction with me was a perfect picture of

God's grace. My Father was reaching out, trying to show me his presence in a moment when all I wanted to do was run from him.

This is the God who would draw me back into his presence many years later. It wasn't the rules or a gavel pronouncing me guilty. I already knew I'd messed up. What I needed to know was that someone loved me despite my mistakes. My inability to follow all the rules is what sent me running away from the church, toward a life of partying, boys, and addictions. I didn't realize how much God cared for me. I didn't realize the lengths he would go to draw me back to himself.

> God's conviction may keep my path straight,
> but it's his grace that keeps me in love.

God's conviction may keep my path straight, but it's his grace that keeps me in love. This is the shift that had to take place in my heart and my view toward God. I had to go from seeing him as distant Rule Enforcer to someone I trusted. From Headmaster and Lecturer to Confidant. Once I understood the type of relationship he desired from me, my life changed. Knowing we are wanted has the capacity to change the entire trajectory of our lives.

When we realize "grace" isn't just some eloquent-sounding word but a gift God wants to give us right where we are, broken rules and all, we're transformed. Our motivation to live in a way that points others to God goes from "have to" to "want to." What I eventually realized was that I wasn't some disobedient kid with a permanent spot on her rap sheet. I was a daughter. I was treasured. And you are too.

On Monday nights I lead a Bible study as part of our church's women's ministry. One night a few months ago, we were talking about the ways God had changed us over the course of an eight-week study we were finishing. A friend in my small group spoke up about how God transformed her view of grace, and as I watched her speak, it was like a veil was being lifted. Her countenance and everything about her demeanor altered, and I thought to myself, "That's what grace does."

Like I did, she had a very legalistic view of God and the church for years. She thought if she could serve enough, fill enough positions in ministry and make everyone happy, God would be happy too. But she lived in a constant state of fear. She dreaded rejection from others and from God, and so she kept both at arm's length. She was afraid if she got too close to anyone, including Jesus, she would be hurt.

Over the course of the study, God did something in her. He changed her. She realized that because she accepted what Jesus did, her place in his family was permanent. Period. End of story. His acceptance had nothing to do with a list of things she had to do or how many ministry titles she had. As his own, she would never be rejected.

In a world that says, "Do," Jesus simply says, "Come." Come as you are. Let my love completely alter your perspective. Leave the checklist.

This type of grace causes a shift in perspective. Instead of being motivated by fear of rejection, we're motivated by trust. But there's another transition that must take place too, and it's one we often overlook. We must let grace transform the way we approach God. Legalism keeps us shackled to our lists and our fear of abandonment, but grace enables us to come to him with hearts full of trust.

This means trusting him even when it doesn't make sense. Even when we're living in our in-laws' basement and we're not sure how long we'll be there. We believe he has a good plan for our future, even when anxiety tries to steal our peace as our home sits on the other side of the country, unsellable.

> Legalism keeps us shackled to our lists and
> our fear of abandonment, but grace enables
> us to come to him with hearts full of trust.

When we approach God with a grace-filled lens, we are confident in his love even when we don't see the solution we'd hoped for. We're still praying and wondering what he's doing, but the transition in our thinking frees us from the heaviness of legalism:

Legalistic Heart:	Grace-Filled Lens:
Fears God has abandoned her	Knows God is for her, even during the wait when she doesn't see the answer
Thinks the lack of a tangible solution means God has left	Knows God loves her no matter what
Distances herself from God when life continues to get hard	Comes to God like a trusted friend through difficulties

As I searched in my in-laws' basement for rental options years ago, I didn't realize I was approaching God with a legalistic view. My trust was limited. I trusted him only as far as my answered prayers took me. But when they weren't answered or I didn't see it, my trust waned.

This isn't what he desires for us. He has something much richer and fuller than a wish-list life. He wants us to know he is good and his plans for us are beautiful, even in the gap of waiting for his response.

In John 15:15, Jesus says, "I no longer call you servants, because a servant does not know his master's business. Instead, I have called you friends, for everything that I learned from my Father I have made known to you." When Jesus tells his disciples everything he learned from his Father, it is an act of trust. For years, I didn't pick up on this distinction. But the more I looked at the passage, the more I saw how significant this declaration was. This intimacy wasn't something he offered to just anyone. If we look at the Pharisees and teachers of the law, we don't see Jesus trusting them in this way. Instead, he speaks to them in parables they don't understand.

By Jesus naming his disciples as friends, he's declaring something special. Something we shouldn't brush past or overlook. If we're his followers, we're his friends too. That means the same trust he extended those first believers is extended to us as well.

> If Jesus trusts us, shouldn't we trust him too?

If Jesus trusts us, shouldn't we trust him too? If he places his confidence in us and whispers secrets straight from heaven, shouldn't we be confident he is going to direct our lives? Even if there are some bumps and surprises?

Throughout Jesus's life, this is the type of relationship he modeled with his Father. There was complete trust. Even though Jesus felt the same emotions we do and displayed frustration at times, he knew there was one thing he could always lean on as infallibly true: his Father's Word.

Jesus's life on earth provides a perfect representation of what our relationship with God can look like. As we look at his interactions with the Father, we see his life wasn't about fulfilling requests from his followers or believers, but about continual communion with his Dad.

Our Blueprint for a Relationship with God

When I first began reading the Gospels, I always found it interesting that we know little about Jesus's life from birth until his earthly ministry began. For approximately thirty years, there isn't much information about what took place. However, there is one account from his childhood in the second chapter of Luke. I overlooked it for years, and it gives some rich insights into Jesus's relationship with his Father.

It starts with Jesus's parents making their annual trip to Jerusalem for the Festival of the Passover. Afterward, they start to return home and travel for a day before they realize Jesus isn't with them. They search anxiously, and finally find their twelve-year-old in the temple courts with the teachers, listening and asking questions. Luke notes everyone was "amazed at his understanding and answers" (Luke 2:47).

Jesus's parents tell him they've been searching for him and note the stress he's caused. He asks, "Why were you searching for me? Didn't you know I had to be in my Father's house?" (Luke 2:49). Although it almost seems like Jesus is being cheeky here, I love how this interaction sets a foundation for what this relationship between Father and Son will be like. To Jesus, it was obvious where he would be because the relationship was vital to who he was.

Jesus didn't just want to be with this Father. He had to be with his Father. His intimacy with him was the cornerstone of his identity, his power, and everything he represented. Without this closeness—the getting away, the prayer, being in his Father's house, and having one-on-one time with him—he couldn't do anything. His work was meaningless.

When I see this picture of their relationship, my approach goes from, "What do I need from him?" to "How can I know him better?" How can I approach the Father in the same way Jesus did? I want to learn and hear from him. My legalistic, wish-list approach is replaced with a desire for closeness.

Jesus's three years of teaching, performing miracles, and healing are marked with repeated times alone with the Father and connecting with him. As I read through the Gospels, paying close attention to his relationship with the Father, I noticed three attributes.

Love, Not Demand

Jesus did not come to serve his needs. He came to do what the Father asked him to do. Although his supernatural acts were important to show he was God, his most important ministry was to love others. Every time he displayed love in action, he gave us a picture of what the Father was like. Before his final meal with his followers, he does a job reserved for the lowest of servants. He washes his disciples' feet.

Can I just be honest here? My own needs can completely blind me to anything else taking place in the world. If there is a crisis situation in my family, it's difficult for me to see other people's needs. And you know what? God cares about each and every concern. For me and for you. But when I start demanding that he provide in a specific way and then get mad when he doesn't, I'm not approaching him with a heart of trust. I'm approaching him like a control freak.

Although we will never completely understand God in this lifetime or know all the reasons for trials and difficulties, it's crucial for a change to take place in our thinking. What he desires most from us isn't sacrifices or service. He wants our hearts and our devotion. He wants our love. A person who loves does not act with manipulation as her motivation.

In his final and most important act of love, Jesus could have saved himself, but he didn't. His greatest gift came not from getting what he wanted, but giving it up. This is how much he loves the Father and loves us. During one of his last interactions with the disciples, he says,

I will not say much more to you, for the prince of
this world is coming. He has no hold over me, but he
comes so that the world may learn that I love the Father
and do exactly what my Father has commanded me.
(John 14:30–31)

Satan knew Jesus's weaknesses and tried to exploit them during those final hours. He knew Jesus longed for another way and tried to make him choose his own desire over the Father's will. But in the end, the enemy's strategy would only serve one purpose: to prove Jesus's devotion to his Father and to us.

Trust over Doubt

I used to think submission to God's will meant lack of desire for a rescue. But the more I looked at Jesus's time in the Garden of Gethsemane, the more I realized I was wrong. Surrender doesn't mean lack of desire for a rescue, but trusting God's way for our lives.

> Surrender doesn't mean lack of desire for a
> rescue, but trusting God's way for our lives.

It means knowing his plans are for our good, even when they're different from our own. It means believing he will be faithful in his promise to give us victory, even when we don't see how victory is possible. We see that no matter what, his grace covers every aspect of our story. Even the difficult times.

Jesus had the benefit of knowing the end of the story. He knew where his home was. And we do too. Although we may not know the details of how our story is going to work out, we know our enemy will not determine the ending. The ending is in God's hands. "The God of peace will soon crush Satan under your feet" (Rom. 16:20).

This knowledge needs to move beyond words on a page and reshape our thinking. Let's say it out loud: "The enemy does not have any power over me. Jesus's love and grace are what will determine my story's ending."

Connection before Action

Each of the Gospels note Jesus's relationship with his Father was marked by repeated time away with him. The fact that he was God did not keep him from prayer and rest in the Father's presence. Before healing many and giving his most famous teaching, the Sermon on the Mount, Luke states Jesus spent an entire night with the Father: "One of those days Jesus went out to a mountainside to pray, and spent the night praying to God" (Luke 6:12).

If Jesus made time away with the Father part of his daily life, I'd venture to say it's even more important for us. Prayer wasn't just a ritual or formula for Jesus. It preceded his power. It prepared the way for action. Our connection to the Father is what will prepare us and equip us for the demands of life as well. Not only that, but it will enable us to keep a perspective of grace instead of being overwhelmed by the troubles surrounding us. When we begin with him instead of coming to him at the end of ourselves, our communication is more like that of a daughter and a friend instead of a distant relative needing an urgent, immediate answer.

The more we get to know him, the more we will see him take us to places we never dreamed possible. But we must take the time to connect and hear from him. Our lives depend on it.

The Prescription for a Breakthrough

It was springtime and buds formed on the bleeding hearts surrounding my in-laws' porch. Their basement was still our home, and now my internal clock was ticking even louder. March brought the announcement of some exciting but terrifying news. Our second child was on the way. Although we found renters for our house in Utah, the hunt for a new home continued.

On Easter Sunday, we attended a local church and when the worship band played, tears fell freely down my cheeks. I realized for months I'd been hiding from my life, afraid to make friends and letting our situation dictate my attitude. I'd been walking around with clenched fists, not seeing the gifts surrounding me. A place to stay during the wait. A family to help us carry the burden while we searched for the right home.

> Surrendering to his will is not a punishment.
> It's my invitation to freedom.

Surrendering to his will is not a punishment. It's my invitation to freedom. In the same way Jesus's surrender to the Father's will brought freedom to us, surrendering to his will for my life brings freedom from worry and anxiety. Freedom from trying to control what I can't control. As the music got louder, I closed my eyes, a spirit of worship overtaking my entire body.

God, I know you have a perfect home for us. I know your plans are for good. Help my unbelief, God. I surrender to the way you have for us. Help me to trust you, even when I don't see the road ahead.

As I left church that day, I had peace. But each day, I struggled to hold onto it and continually had to commit myself to trust. It is not something that came naturally, but a decision I made each day. I took our firstborn to visit my parents in South Carolina, hoping the distance away would calm my nerves. My husband stayed north and continued searching for homes while we were gone.

In early May, we visited a house that sat on top of a mountain. I fell in love with the neighborhood, the view, and the cul-de-sac street. I knew it would be a perfect location for our growing family. But it needed a lot of TLC. The paint in the living room was chipping and wires hung from the ceiling where the light fixtures once were. Where I saw work, my husband saw potential. He saw a home and years of memories.

Two weeks later, we made an offer on the house; and after a couple of negotiations, we received the call from our realtor. It wasn't simply a house anymore. It was home. The wait was finally over.

When June arrived and we were putting fresh paint on the walls, I stopped for a break and stepped out onto the deck behind the house. Out of the corner of my eye, I saw a rabbit hop by, looking for his next meal. He stopped and sniffed his surroundings, whiskers twitching right and left. I smiled knowing I would witness sights like this on a regular basis. And I realized something. In all my months of waiting and worrying, God was preparing a perfect place for us.

While I thought he was withholding, he was waiting to give us abundance. Months before moving I had spotted this house on a real estate website, but the price was out of our range. During the time we stayed at my in-laws', the owner came down on his price.

Only God.

Now, when I come to him with my prayers and desires, I approach him with confidence. Our time in the basement changed me. I see that giving him my prayers with open hands doesn't mean a lack of want. It doesn't mean bracing myself for punishment. It's an act of belief and assurance in who he is. It's knowing he wants to give me more than I could think to ask for.

He's that good of a Father. Jesus knew this. And as his children, we can too.

Adjusting Our Lens

1. Is your approach to God a long list of expectations, or do you come with a desire to know him as a person? What would it look like to come to him desiring connection and relationship instead of an action item? Today, sit in his presence and just be. See what he lays on your heart.

2. How did your upbringing impact your personal view of God? Do you see him as a distant dictator or as a friend? How do you think viewing him as a friend would impact your faith and spiritual walk? Spend some time talking to him as a friend today. See how it affects your view of him.

3. Do you think of surrender to God's will as punishment or an invitation to freedom? If you view it as punishment, what do you think he may withhold from you if you surrender? Take some time to identify what's holding you back. Then, confess it. Give it to God.

9

When "No" Is God's Saving Grace

"No" isn't a word I like using often. Somewhere in my life, I adapted the belief that "yes" is synonymous with love. I once took a personality test that matched personality type with an animal. Mine was a cross between a golden retriever and a beaver. Crazy to envision, I know. But when I moved past the picture in my head, what it broke down to was something like this: "Let me make you happy and work hard so I can feel needed and valued." The problem is, sometimes I "yes" myself into a stress-filled life where the only person I'm helping is my ego.

There are times when I project the helper part of my personality onto God too. If he's saying yes to my prayers, requests, and felt needs, I see him as my biggest advocate. But when those periods of waiting and noes come, I wonder if he's helping me at all.

God is working on my heart in this area; and several months ago, I realized my vision was skewed. I read through the Gospel of John, and I saw how I often I cast this "yes equals love" mentality onto my Father. Somehow and perhaps unwittingly, I misconstrued Jesus's words in John about sending a Helper to mean sending someone who will say yes when I think it's best.

What I didn't see is that God's "no" is just as much a product of his grace as his "yes" is. His "no" can correct our course, redirect us, keep us from danger, and prevent us from looking like fools. It can prepare us and strengthen us from the season when yeses come like clockwork and we question our ability to handle the pressure and expectations of those around us. But most of the time, instead of seeing his "no" as an opportunity for growth or rest, we see it as discipline or a sign that he isn't for us. Much like my two-year-old daughter screams mercilessly when I don't give in to her demands, we often think our ways are better than his ways.

Remember all those years we carried two mortgages, renting a house on the other side of the country? There were many times I went to the Lord begging him to release us from that burden. One season, we went three months without a rental payment. Another year, the renters vacated the house without giving any notice, leaving the place in need of numerous repairs. As our bank account and minimal savings got lower, my blood pressure became higher. My husband and I felt the tension growing in our marriage as we felt completely helpless to expedite our growing need for additional income.

When we decided to cut our losses and list the house, it didn't sell. With each day that passed, I became aware that my will and God's were not the same. And as much as I tried to bend his arm a little and manipulate him into seeing things my way, the answer remained the same. For a long, difficult season, it was hard for me to see God. Although I kept coming to him, it became less and less often. There was a noticeable barrier between us. At the time, I didn't understand why my prayers felt lifeless and dead. I didn't realize my response to what I perceived as a "no" from him was affecting our relationship.

This is why it's critical that we recognize our responses to this despised word. Because in order for us to shift the way we see it, we must become conscious of our natural reactions to it.

How We Respond to "No"

Although there are many varied ways we can respond to "no," and they will differ depending on our personalities, relationship with God, and life experiences, we are only going to look at three because most of the time, they fall into one or more of these categories. My hope is that by understanding our reactions, we will be better equipped to recognize when we drift from our relationship and his truth.

1. We Become Angry

One of the most common ways we respond to a "no" or a "wait" that's perceived as a "no" is to become angry. My two-year-old daughter is living proof. It's her least favorite word on the entire planet, unless she's the one saying it. No other quick, single-syllable utterance can set off her temper in one second flat and keep her screaming for fifteen minutes after the conversation is over. And although as adults we may not throw tantrums or cry at the top of our lungs, we never quite grow out of our dislike for the word.

For most of us living in America or any first-world country, we're told we can have it all. Need to slim up for swimsuit season or lose twenty pounds? There's a five-minute workout, pill, or wrap to meet your needs. Need to spruce up your wardrobe? According to your latest email promotions, you "must have" this new line of clothing. With expedited shipping and instant posting on social media channels, our culture doesn't often hear about the value in waiting or being told no. What good could come of it?

So is it any wonder why we become angry when we receive a "no" from God? Can't he see this request is something we need or want with every part of our being? Yes, he does. But he also sees what waits for us on the other side of his "yes" or "no."

2. We Become Distant

This is what happened to me all those months when our house sat without a buyer. I thought it was God who became distant. I was wrong. And what I eventually recognized was this: God doesn't alter his position in our lives. We alter our position to him.

We equate "no" with an uncaring, remote Father, so our prayers become less frequent. We think a "no" means he doesn't want to hear our requests, so we stop bringing them to him. Like the silent treatments we used to give our friends when we became mad in middle school, we give God the cold shoulder.

After all, wouldn't a loving Father who truly saw what we were going through be concerned for our needs? We will talk about this more, but the answer is yes. Always.

3. We Take Matters into Our Own Hands

If it's within our power to do so, sometimes we ignore what God has to say. I admit I've done this on several occasions. And as much as I tried to pretend like I wasn't aware of what God was speaking to my heart or plead ignorance to his voice, I knew. When peace left and stress prevailed in my life, I knew it even more.

Women and men have a long history of taking things into their hands when God says no to something. Even though I've heard it hundreds of times since I was a kid in Vacation Bible School, I'm always drawn to the stories in Genesis. Particularly the story of

Adam and Eve. This is where it all began, right? Where the course of history and our relationship with God was changed forever.

Although the wisdom and knowledge we can glean from Genesis 3 is as endless as our Creator himself, what always strikes me as I read it is this: God says no, and we assume he's withholding something from us. Despite the fact that Eve wasn't present when God gave the command not to eat of the Tree of Knowledge of Good and Evil, she knew the tree was forbidden. She even goes so far as to exaggerate God's command and say they must not touch it either, although it's unclear where she received this overstated information. Despite her awareness, she eats. "When the woman saw that the fruit of the tree was good for food and pleasing to the eye, and also desirable for gaining wisdom, she took some and ate it" (Gen. 3:6). Sure, the serpent came along and lured Eve into deceit. He fooled her into believing she lacked something, even though she was perfect. But here's the key—she believed him. What we believe about God will always impact how we respond to his yes and his no.

So, the question is—what do we believe? Do we believe he is for us, even when hope is deferred and we don't understand his decision? Do we believe he sees not only the obstacle we're fixated on right now, but also our future?

There have been times when I let the control freak in me take over. I thought my plan was the best one, and I could see in my mind's eye how beautifully everything would turn out if each detail went exactly according to my formula. Then, life happened. In one circumstance after another, I found myself lying flat on my face, asking, "What now, God?" All of my perfectly laid plans were strewn out around me, a mess of chaos and broken dreams. I felt as though my security blanket had been ripped out from under me and thrown into the fire.

In a moment of endless questions and doubts, I called on God and he answered me. He led me to a passage I'd read many times, but it came to life in a new way. I found myself walking in the Garden of Gethsemane with Jesus, mere hours before his death. He became more human to me than ever before.

Taking It to the One Who Knows

When you read Jesus's final plea to his Father, one thing is strikingly evident: his will is separate from his Father's. Although his purpose was to do the will of the One who sent him, he always had a choice. God didn't send an android or a celestial being devoid of feelings and desires, but a person. A human who had wants and impulses just like you and me. He had the ability to say no as easily as he could say yes.

> For we do not have a high priest who is unable to empathize with our weaknesses, but we have one who has been tempted in every way, just as we are—yet he did not sin. (Heb. 4:15)

While I think most of us know this truth in our heads because we've read it and heard it many times, I'm not sure most of us actually see Jesus this way. We see him performing miracles, living a sinless life, and doing everything the Father asked him to do. We see what separates him rather than what made him like us.

It's important we acknowledge him as holy and set apart because he is each of these things, but I think it's also crucial that we see that he was human. Because the human part of him is the part we can relate to as he cries out to God, sweats drops of blood, and experiences true anguish over what's about to happen. The human part of him is the one who begs his Father for deliverance and another way, even when he knows in his Spirit there is no other way.

When we acknowledge that Jesus was human and can relate to us during those times when we're frustrated, angry, or disappointed because we don't understand God's response, we can connect with him on a deeper level. Remembering he experienced each of the struggles we do, we can . . .

1. Approach him with confidence, knowing he understands, even if the answer doesn't change.
2. Approach him with gratitude, knowing he intercedes on our behalf and makes our needs known to the Father.
3. Approach him with certainty, knowing he sees us and acknowledges each detail of our situation, knowing he will equip us to face it no matter what the outcome is.

Even though Jesus wanted to be delivered from the pain he anticipated in the coming hours, you and I know the end of the story. There was no other way. Jesus had to go to the cross, for you and for me. This is how much God desired a relationship with us.

> God's no to his only Son in one moment
> equaled a yes to us for all eternity.

God's no to his only Son in one moment equaled a yes to us for all eternity. Sit for a moment and wrap your head around the significance of those words. By choosing not to grant his son's last request here on earth, he welcomed you and I in to sit at the table with the King of Kings. The veil dividing us was broken from top to bottom. Each one of our lives was forever changed, and we were given a choice we never had before: the freedom to choose him. The unmatched gift of being able to choose Jesus, who ended his prayer by saying, "yet not my will, but yours be done" (Luke 22:42).

Can you imagine what our lives would have looked like if the Father had said yes? Don't you think he wished there was another solution to our eternal problem? I look at my own kids and think about how hard it is for me to say no even when I'm certain it's better for them in the long run. I can't even fathom saying no if it meant seeing them experience pain.

But even though the cup wasn't taken from Jesus, we still see how much the Father loved the Son. He didn't leave Jesus to grieve by himself. He sent relief and comfort: "An angel from heaven appeared to him and strengthened him" (Luke 22:43).

When his answer is no, God still sends comfort. He sends relief to build us up during our time of need. If you're facing what seems like an impossible situation right now, keep looking for his mercies. He does not leave us to go through it alone.

Looking Past an Answer

Seeing Jesus die wasn't what the Jews wanted either. They wanted a king. They wanted someone who was going to deliver them from the oppression they were facing at the hands of the Roman Empire. Even at a young age, before he had performed any miracles or started his earthly ministry, people came from afar to worship him as king.

> After Jesus was born in Bethlehem in Judea, during
> the time of King Herod, Magi from the east came to
> Jerusalem and asked, "Where is the one who has been
> born king of the Jews? We saw his star when it rose and
> have come to worship him. (Matt. 2:1–2)

But a king who would let himself be killed for a crime he didn't commit? A humble servant who would wash feet the night before he died and refuse to say a word to defend himself when soldiers led him to Golgotha? No, this is not what they had in mind. Not at all.

By not giving his people what they wanted, Jesus gave them what they needed most. He gave them rest for their souls. He gave them deliverance. Not from an earthly ruler, but from the enemy who tries to steal our hearts and distract our minds. If Jesus had decided to sacrifice himself only to overthrow a temporary ruler, you and I would have no hope for this world or the next. If he'd bended to the Jews' will and defeated Rome, he only would have provided a solution to a momentary problem. And eventually, another empire would rise. Another persecutor would take leadership.

Sometimes by saying no, Jesus is giving us something better than we could even imagine. He's opening his hands and allowing us access to a gift we've never thought to hope for. Not seeing him work in the way we wanted allows us to see him in a whole new way. Eventually, those who came to know him and believe in him saw that instead of becoming King of the Jews, Jesus became King of All. King of Heaven and Earth. He completed his work here, rose from the dead, and sat down at the right hand of the Father. This ending is not one anyone envisioned. It was beyond their wildest wonder. It was mind-blowing to the millionth degree.

The more we realize Jesus is unlimited, able to care for us even when it seems to go against everything we think we need, the more we can believe he's good both in the noes and the yeses. The more we can trust that his faithfulness goes beyond an answer, and is not limited by what we see today.

The Blessing of No

I am the absolute worst person to try to surprise with anything. Ask anyone who knows me well. My husband will be the first to tell you, trying to surprise me will turn into your worst nightmare. Whether it's a gift or a party, it never quite works out as planned.

At my questioning, my mom told me Santa wasn't real when I was ten years old. My brother is six years older than I and kept me on my toes, so the story of a fat man climbing down chimneys was kind of hard to wrap my head around anyway. Once the make-believe was over, my parents just put all the presents under our ginormous tree once they were wrapped. Bad idea. To be honest, I'm not sure what they were thinking. So, my brother and I would carefully pull back the tape of our presents and peek, making sure to put the corners of the wrapping paper back in their original positions.

When I got married, my husband quickly realized how devious I was, and once we started buying gifts for each other, he made one thing clear. Several, actually. No peeking. No shaking. No touching. You get the picture. Once, when he noticed I had moved a gift that he'd placed under the tree by a quarter of an inch, he later told me he'd taken it back to the store. He hadn't, but, needless to say, I never touched another gift again.

This particular Christmas was our first one as a married couple and we were spending it at my in-laws' house. When he brought me my gift in the morning after all the other presents had been opened, I was like a kid all over again as I tore my way through a series of "ahas." And inside a piece of luggage I'd been eying, there was a pearl necklace. The final gift he'd been hiding for weeks. He remembered how I borrowed my mother's for our wedding day, and wanted me to have my own. It was the perfect finale to months of asking for hints and being told no. An unanticipated ending to what I thought I had made into a disaster.

By saying no to what I wanted, he gave me a gift I didn't expect. And the not knowing is what made it special. It's what made it worth the wait.

Many times, when I approach God, I'm like the little girl on Christmas Eve. I want to know what he's doing and see the plans that haven't unfolded yet. I want to see the answers now instead of waiting for this timing, even though I can look back and see how he hasn't failed me before. But because he's a good Father, he says, "No. Not yet, my child." And waiting can be frustrating. Grueling, at times.

But the more I commit to looking for him even when I'm frustrated, the more he shows up in ways I couldn't envision. He answers prayers. He gives gifts I don't deserve.

When our house in Utah finally sold, we were on a summer camping trip with friends. Chris and I drove around a tiny town in northern New York looking for a notary and a place to overnight the papers back to the title company. We would've driven for hours if we'd needed to. We couldn't get the documents signed fast enough.

That same week, my proposal for my first book was getting pitched to publishers. It was a goal I'd been working toward for over four years, and there had been times I'd wondered if I was wasting my time. I'd spent a couple of years in the place Seth Godin refers to as "the dip," with the thrill of a new dream behind me but with my goal continuing to elude me.

Then, the same day our house sold, I was sitting in our camper, feeding our daughter before putting her to bed. When she finally dozed off, I picked up my phone to check emails and noticed one from my agent. The subject line said the words I'd been waiting years to hear. We had an offer. A publisher was interested in my book. Not only that, they were excited about it.

Some may call it coincidence. I know it wasn't. It was God cupping my face in his hands and saying, "Remember all those prayers to you spoke to me? All those times you thought I said no? I heard every single one."

As I sat there in our camper, all I could do was whisper one thank you after another. To say I was amazed is an understatement. I could barely articulate the news to my husband because of my complete awe over what God had done.

God doesn't stop working when we're frustrated or angry. He's full of grace and mercy, and he knows what's good for us better than anyone. Sometimes he says no. Although I don't think he expects us to like it, I do know he wants us to trust him. He wants us to keep thanking him, even when it's hard.

Why? Because when we do, it changes us. The roots of our faith grow deep because instead of being dependent on an answer, they're dependent on a person who doesn't change. His no is good and his yes is good because it's impossible for him to be anything less.

No matter what his answer is today, know he's aware of each detail of your circumstance. He is not annoyed by your requests or your needs, but attentive to each one.

Adjusting Our Lens

1. Is there an area of your life where God is saying "no" or "not yet?" What could he be saying "yes" to right now?
2. Look at the desires of your heart and ask yourself how God's "no" could allow you to see him more clearly as a Provider, a Counselor, and a Friend.

10

The Faith We Find in Staying

Often, it's easy to see God at the beginning of a new project, leap of faith, or move. The rush of enthusiasm is present with each step and our heart beats fast with an eagerness to begin each day. But then we get to the middle. We get to the part where hard work and reality set in, distractions come, and we question ourselves. We may question God too.

Moving and starting a new thing can become an addiction. Just ask someone who's moved several times. Whether it's relocating to a new town, starting a new job, or setting out on a fresh adventure, there's nothing like the thrill of beginnings.

Nearly a year ago, I felt God calling me to start a women's Bible study at our church. It was a rather new plant we'd been attending for five years, and although they periodically had women's events such as luncheons with speakers and other activities, they had never had a women's Bible study. As I listened to the needs of friends and attendees, I knew they were thirsty for one. So, I approached the pastor's wife with an eight-week, DVD-based study God led me to with much prayer, and, albeit with apprehension, I volunteered to lead it.

She and I met for dinner one night to discuss the details, and she shared with me how my text message was an answer to prayer. For months, she'd been praying for a woman to rise up and take leadership in the church, and she knew my desire was also God's way of showing her he was listening.

I drove home that evening thanking God and praising him for his confirmation. For weeks before it began, I committed to praying for the women who would attend the study, and I was pumped to begin. At our first meeting, we had over forty women attend. Each of them was eager to dig in and learn. Each of them was excited to see what God would do over the course of the next two months.

But several weeks in, the numbers dwindled. Kids' baseball games started and other activities beckoned. The weekly readings weren't done, and when I prompted the women with questions about what they learned, I was met with blank stares. As much as I tried to remain focused and remember the passion I felt at the beginning, I was discouraged. Some weeks, I was tempted to phone it in or ask another member of the church if she could lead.

In those moments when I wondered if any of the time I was investing was making a difference and longed for another fresh start, I had to practice what I've come to know as staying faith.

Staying faith means continuing to work through our current situation, even when the well appears to be dry.

This is the type of faith that makes us stay put when we are tempted to make the next move before God's timing or long for the promise of new beginnings again. It's the kind of hope that keeps us devoted to the place we are, even when we don't see fruit. It requires us to shift our focus from what we feel to what we know—that God has called us and equipped us.

In Galatians, Paul describes it like this: "Let us not become weary of doing good, for at the proper time we will reap a harvest if we do not give up" (Gal. 6:9). Although I felt defeated at times during those two months, I knew I was where God wanted me to be. I knew I had to keep my mind centered on this truth and remain as committed in the middle of the study as I was in the beginning. So this is what I did. And eventually, I realized his presence was still there.

Becoming a mom was the practicing ground that taught me what staying faith was. During the mornings when I had no clue what I was doing and believed a monkey could do a better job of taking care of our son, I continued to put one foot in front of the other. I got up and tried to be the mother my son needed, even on the restless nights when I felt like crying right along with him.

I once told my husband it was no wonder that many new moms experience postpartum depression. For months, they're filled with anticipation of what's to come and are the center of attention. Everything from their weight, diet, cravings, and hormones are under constant scrutiny. They're celebrated with showers and celebrations of coming life. The countdown is on as they shop for the perfect nursery décor and outfits for the baby to wear during their first weeks.

Then the baby comes, and everything changes. The anticipation is over, and the focus shifts from mom to baby. She's thrown, somewhat bewildered, into months of sleepless nights, midnight diaper explosions, and feedings, all while trying to heal and figure out what she's doing. And while motherhood is a role filled with moments of joy, it is also one of the most self-sacrificing jobs there is.

When new beginnings and expectancy turn to endless days of the same, the transition can be grueling. We must get up each day and make the choice to be present. We must find those new moments and opportunities for joy, even when they seem hidden.

I experienced postpartum depression in varying degrees after each one of my births, but the first one was by far the most severe. It felt like I was trying to wade through quicksand, and as much as I wanted to take in all the new life that was in front of me, all I wanted to do was crawl into bed when my husband came home from work.

Chris had to learn staying faith too. When he wasn't sure what happened to the wife he married and wanted nothing more than for my joy to return, he had to believe things would get better. He had to believe the God who brought us to this place would help us navigate through this season of newness mixed with isolation. He had to remain constant and steady.

> Sometimes staying in the place God gives us takes more faith than moving the mountain.

Sometimes staying in the place God gives us takes more faith than moving the mountain. There are times in life when God calls us to leap or make a bold move for him. It takes every ounce of confidence we have in him in order to do what he's asking us to do and take down a mountain that seems insurmountable. But there are other seasons when he tells us to keep our feet firmly planted where he has us. And in these chapters of life, our faith is stretched in different ways.

Looking Past Endless Distractions

When I think of men and women in the Bible who illustrated the power of staying faith, one name comes to mind: Nehemiah.

Nehemiah knew what it meant to remain diligent in the task God gave him to do, but he also faced constant obstacles and distractions.

His job? It was to rebuild the wall surrounding Jerusalem, which was a pile of rubble. The gates had been burned, and the Jews who were assimilating back into the land after years in captivity had no protection from their enemies. Nehemiah was distraught about the state of his homeland, and his mission required a team who would not only help construct the wall, but also ward off opposition who came to fight and distract the builders.

I imagine when Nehemiah first set out to complete his assignment, he was filled with purpose and the vigor of a fresh vision from the Lord. Before leaving for Jerusalem, he was a cupbearer to the Persian king. He needed the king's approval to leave his post, and spent days fasting and praying before approaching him. Can you imagine the fear and the nerves he felt when he brought the king his wine, thinking of what he would say? King Artaxerxes could have taken Nehemiah's life with one word, and the mere fact that he allowed him to go was a miracle.

But to keep working for the Lord at such a daunting, arduous task in the midst of continual resistance requires more than excitement. Because once you get past the rush of starting, you're faced with the work. And the work Nehemiah had to do was backbreaking. Not only that, but he and his team were also distracted by those who wanted them to fail. The adrenaline of the launch faded even more quickly.

Staying faith requires recognizing that the messy middle is just as important as the beginning. This is exactly what Nehemiah did. Despite the hurdles he encountered day after day, he didn't quit. Despite being constantly taunted and ridiculed by those who opposed their work and their mission, he and his team stayed right where God had them, even though their lives were at risk. They stayed on guard not only during the day while they were working, but also at night.

> At that time I also said to the people, "Have every man and his helper stay inside Jerusalem at night, so they can serve us as guards by night and as workers by day." Neither I nor my brothers nor my men nor the guards with me took off our clothes; each had his weapon, even when he went for water. (Neh. 4:22–23)

So what was Nehemiah's secret? How did he continue to stay persistent and faithful to his mission despite never-ending barriers? As I read through this story, there were a few attributes of this prophet that stood out.

> Staying faith requires recognizing that the messy middle is just as important as the beginning.

1. Recognition of the Goal

Nehemiah knew exactly what his mission was. He didn't question it or second-guess it. He was prayed up and sure of God's calling when he approached the king, and the king's approval served to only further his resolve. So when obstacles came, Nehemiah knew it wasn't because he'd picked the wrong course. He knew it wasn't because God was against him or had abandoned him. He recognized the setback for what it was: a distraction from the enemy.

Sticking to the work God assigned us doesn't mean it's going to go according to our plan. But it does mean he'll be with us. It means his purpose will prevail, even if it means working through miles of rubble and ash to see it.

When we keep our eyes fixed on the goal, we can move past interruptions without letting them completely derail us. We can see them as bumps in the path instead of complete changes to it.

Sometimes, when we don't see the swift outcome we want, we can become discouraged. The temptation to abandon ship or start on the next new thing can be great. This is what happened when I led the women's Bible study at our church. I started it with plenty of energy and excitement over what God would do. I studied hard, prayed harder, and couldn't wait for Mondays each week.

At first, most of the ladies who attended seemed equally enthusiastic. But as the study progressed, I didn't get the feedback I anticipated and assumed silence meant the worst. I knew it was a busy time of year and kids' activities, family schedules, and other responsibilities beckoned, but feelings of failure overwhelmed me.

One day, I had to make a decision. I had to shift my focus from personal feelings and expectations to my goal. And my goal was to finish the work God gave me to do. Regardless of how I felt, I was sure of one thing. He had called me. So I pressed on.

2. Recognition of the Enemy

In order to press forward, I had to employ the same tactic Nehemiah did when he rebuilt the wall. I had to know my enemy.

Nehemiah's enemy may seem more obvious. After all, they openly plotted to kill him and his army while delivering messages of threats and insults. But while it may not have been hard for Nehemiah to recognize who they were, he did have to continually remember an aspect of their character others may have overlooked. They were not God.

They could intimidate, but they couldn't overthrow. They could talk a big talk, but they couldn't intercept the prayers being delivered to the Lord.

Our enemy may look completely different. It may look like self-defeating talk or doubt. It may look like someone who doesn't understand our calling, who repeatedly voices her opinion. The details of each scenario will be different, but one truth will remain the same: our adversary will be a voice contrary to God's.

When we identify our enemy, we can also claim victory over him. We become aware of his methods and the buttons he pushes.

This awareness played a huge part in Nehemiah's success, and it is what kept him working without interruption when interference came. Even when new tactics were employed to try to get him to leave the wall and meet with officials who would sidetrack his efforts, he did not fall for their deceit: "I am carrying on a great project and cannot go down. Why should the work stop while I leave it and go down to you?" (Neh. 6:3).

3. Recognition of Our Defender

Nehemiah knew if God wasn't part of this project, it would be a complete failure. He also knew if God didn't protect his men and keep the enemy at bay, they would all be dead. He repeatedly came to God in prayer and reminded the builders who held their victory in his hands: "Don't be afraid of them. Remember the Lord, who is great and awesome, and fight for your families, your sons and your daughters, your wives and your homes" (Neh. 4:14).

When we want to abandon a task God has given us or start over, it's often because we're relying on our own strength instead of his. We're trying to control outcomes and put our hands on every detail, when he is the one who is ultimately in charge of the conclusion. And while he wants us to be diligent and to be good stewards of the work he's given us, there will always be elements that are beyond our ability to control.

Nehemiah couldn't control the army of people who rose up against them, but he could depend on God and equip his men to defend themselves. He couldn't make others see the value of the work they were doing, but he knew God did.

When we know who our Defender is, we can keep pressing forward with confidence, even when difficulties rise. We can be tenacious in the face of overwhelming odds because we know we serve a God who protects us not with swords and shields, but with a host of angels who work in unseen places.

God of the Middle

When we stay faithful in the messy middle, God does something beautiful in us. He builds strength and resolve in our hearts that keeps us centered in his truth when hard seasons come. Our decision to remain steadfast becomes a deposit we will use later during times life doesn't make sense.

Nehemiah and his people finished their wall. The Jews finally had a place where they could lay down in safety and rebuild the lives they lost when their families were taken into captivity. Because he was faithful in each stage of the process and was as diligent midway through it as he was in the beginning, God rewarded him. Future generations of Jews would be impacted by his perseverance.

Remember the church where I led the Bible study? Did I mention it was in a basement? For years, my pastor and his wife leased part of a building that was right in the middle of downtown Cumberland, which is exactly where they felt God calling them to plant a church several years before. One of my pastor's good friends referred to it as "the beacon in the basement," and that is what we were for many years.

Our town suffers from widespread drug addiction, fatal overdoses, poverty, and people lacking any glimmer of hope, but we were a light pointing others to God's truth. However, a basement wasn't where our church wanted to be. There was no sunlight in the building and there were people who wouldn't attend because of claustrophobia. With church shootings on the rise, some worried that we didn't have a safe way to escape if catastrophe hit. Most of all, we didn't have space to grow. The youth ministry met in a tiny room that would have been better suited for a coat closet.

Even though the location had its shortcomings, it was exactly where God kept our church for five years. Every time our pastor and other church leaders would look for another place to establish their church, they were disappointed. They worried about the needs of their congregation and wondered how long God would keep them in a place where they couldn't thrive in all the ways they wanted to. But even though questions without answers abounded, they were faithful. They kept showing up, week after week, and doing the work God had called them to do.

In spring of 2018, God delivered a miracle. A Wesleyan church about five miles from the basement location had been abandoned, and the building was for sale. Even though there was no seller contact information anywhere on the property, our pastor was able to locate a leader in the Wesleyan church within an hour. The two men immediately made a connection, and it was obvious God's hand was in each detail. Within a month, the building was sold. We had a new home with plenty of space to grow, host events, and build our ministry.

Sometimes the middle ground takes years to walk through. It can be frustrating. It can feel like you're moving in circles and not making any progress. But when we keep seeking God and remain steadfast in the place he has us, he delivers. He keeps using us and works in ways we may not even see when we're in it.

Fruits of Middle Ground Faithfulness

It was spring when we reached the end of the first women's Bible study at our church. To be honest, I was tired and ready for a break.

For weeks I'd carried the weight of discouragement on my shoulders, although I knew God was asking me to give it to him. So, in the days leading up to our meeting, I prayed those who had been absent for the last several weeks would return and take part in the fellowship. I surrendered to God what I couldn't control, and committed to taking the steps I could to making our last meeting a success.

I reached some whose contact information I had, and posted updates about our final get-together on our group Facebook page. To celebrate the end of our study, we planned a potluck and let those who were willing share testimonies of what God had done throughout the past couple of months. Instead of breaking into small groups after the DVD and teaching portion, like we normally did, the entire group stayed together and discussed the wrap-up questions.

As I sat there listening to the responses from these women who had become friends, all I could do was praise God. Despite my mid-study feelings of defeat, God had been working the whole time. He had been moving in hearts, and the truth of his Word was giving freedom to several who had been living stuck in destructive thought patterns and habits. Even during the moments when I doubted whether this commitment was making a difference, his Spirit was transforming lives and equipping them to fight battles I didn't even know were taking place.

> When God calls us to do something, he doesn't leave us once we reach the middle of the task.

When God calls us to do something, he doesn't leave us once we reach the middle of the task. He doesn't say, "Well, it looks like she has this under control, so I'm going to go help this other person." He stays. He uses us in ways we can't conceive. He's the faithful God of the beginning, the middle, and the end.

Often, the middle requires us to get our hands dirty. It may mean doing things we're not comfortable doing or could look different than we visualized when we first began. But when we practice staying faith and let the same God who filled us with fire at the starting line keep the fire burning through the middle and the end, lives are changed. Like the Jews who followed Nehemiah and his builders, lives could be transformed for generations to come.

Don't let the messiness of the middle keep you from finishing the work God called you to do. Keep looking for his presence in the details. Keep working like he's right there beside you. Because he is. And one day, you will see the fruit he brought forth in that place.

Adjusting Our Lens

1. Is there an area of your life where God may be asking you to finish the work you started? How can you guard the time you have to work on this task and prevent distractions?

2. On a piece of paper, draw three or more circles, with a few inches between each one, representing major milestones in your life, such as graduating from college, getting that position you really wanted, taking a leap of faith for the Lord, or starting a family. Label each one with events that were important to you. Between each one, draw one or two smaller circles. In them, write some of the seemingly less significant events that led up to the milestone ones. Such events may include passing your midterm exams, waiting in prayer for God to move, submitting résumés, etc. As you look at what you've written down on these smaller circles, do they seem less significant, or do you see how they created a foundation for what was to come? Why or why not?

11

How We Gain the Clearest View of God

If we wanted to see all the highlights of the island, we needed to take a helicopter ride. This is what our travel agent and everyone who'd visited Kauai told us before we left for our honeymoon. Of course, we wanted to witness all the sights we'd seen in magazines firsthand, like the Na'Pali Coast and Waimaea Canyon. The kid in me was counting down the days like a five-year-old waiting for Christmas Eve. So, several months before our wedding, I booked a tour.

I still remember how I could feel the adrenaline coursing through me as the pilot lifted the aircraft up and I could see the coastline for miles and miles. I'd never experienced anything like it. Being in the air allowed us to see the island from a completely different perspective, and the ground we were able to cover in mere seconds gave us a new appreciation for its beauty.

While the high aerial view was spectacular, there was one part of the island where the pilot had to lower the aircraft into a valley in order for us to see its grandeur. It's known as the second wettest place on earth, and its summit reaches toward the sky in a circular shape, almost mimicking the crater of a volcano with an opening inviting the flyer into the center. This mountain is called Wai'ale'ale, which literally means "ripping water" or "overflowing water."[1] As the pilot made his way down into the valley, we saw why. Stretching up thousands of feet above us on nearly every side were waterfalls covering a lush, green landscape. It was straight out of a scene from a movie, which is no mistake because many movies, including *Jurassic Park*, were filmed there. No words quite do justice to the sight we witnessed. It took my breath away, and I sat there transfixed by God's creation surrounding me from every angle.

But you know what? If the pilot hadn't lowered the helicopter into this ravine, we would've missed it. To appreciate the beauty that came from above, we had to be willing to go down below. We had to not only trust the captain to get us safely in and out of this area, but we had to have faith that he knew the island better than we did. And because we believed each of these things, the payoff was stunning. My husband and I each experienced a moment we will never forget, and it was a result of our letting go of control.

The entire experience is a picture of what God has taught me over ten years of following him through the valleys, the mountaintops, and everything in between. I used to think I would see more of God with promotion and success. By achieving goals, building platforms, and proving myself to everyone. We live in a culture obsessed with showing the best version of ourselves to the world. Take the selfie after securing the job opportunity. Check. Post all the highlights of our days, whether we're tired, lonely, or grief-stricken. Check. Let others see the triumphs, but keep the failures hidden. Double check.

But the more I seek him, the more I find that God isn't concerned with platforms and appearances. He desires humble offerings made with our hands open. Sometimes he places us on a stage and other times he puts us in a valley, but our ability to see him is the same in either place. If we want to see God, the question we should be asking ourselves isn't how can I get promoted, but how can I serve?

> If we want to see God, the question we should be asking ourselves isn't how can I get promoted, but how can I serve?

The Posture of a Servant

Jesus gave up everything when he came to earth. Scripture tells us he was with the Father at the beginning when heaven and earth were created, and every bit of it was made by him and for him (Col. 1:16). He lacked no good thing, yet he lowered himself. Not because he needed us, but because he desired us. So, he gave up his position and made himself a servant. A servant who would walk with the poor, heal the lame and the sick, and touch people who had been outcasts for years. He would wash feet and converse with every type of sinner. Jesus's view of the Father was the greatest not when he used his position for his own advantage. As a matter of fact, he never did this, even in the face of torture and death. Instead, his vision of the Father remained clear and unblemished because he humbled himself in complete obedience.

Those who were considered the highest on the totem pole of righteousness and authority were actually criticized by Jesus more than anyone else in Scripture. They were the Pharisees, and Jesus immediately saw that their actions were not those of people who truly desired to know God or serve him, but were rooted in shallow, self-serving motivation. They wanted to be seen as moral but were empty on the inside. They desired status, but did not desire God. Jesus was quick to point out the discrepancy between their inner and outer selves when he dined with a Pharisee, and the man questioned him about not washing before the meal.

> Now then, you Pharisees clean the outside of the
> cup and dish, but inside you are full of greed and
> wickedness. You foolish people! Did not the one who
> made the outside make the inside also? (Luke 11:39–40)

The motivation leading our hearts will always spill over into our actions. If we want to look successful to others but aren't seeking God, our life's trajectory will eventually lead us nowhere. We will reach the place where we thought we'd find happiness, only to find there's nothing but empty, fading praise that's here today and gone tomorrow.

Remember Mount Wai'ale'ale? Although Chris and I saw spectacular views once the pilot lowered the helicopter down into the valley, the top of the mountain was barren. It had been pummeled for years by excessive rainfall, wind, and the elements. There was practically no life there; and while it was still beautiful in its own unique way, it could not sustain the lush, green growth covering the area below it.

Our drive in life is often like this mountain we saw twelve years ago. While God honors ambition and goals, there is no peak of success in our time on earth where life can be sustained. A valley of some sort, whether physical or spiritual, will always follow. There is a certain weight that comes with achievement, and if we're not continually seeking God and abiding in his will for us, it often burdens our souls with a heaviness we were never intended to carry.

The Weight of Success

Well-known pastor, author, and speaker Francis Chan knows the difference between the satisfaction worldly promotion brings and joy that is soul deep. Several years ago, he walked away from a megachurch he'd planted in California that had over five thousand people attending each week. He'd written a best-selling book, had his face on the cover of magazines, and was a sought-after speaker, but something didn't feel right. He didn't believe it was what God was calling him to do. He had all the accolades any person could want and a church that was thriving by American standards, but he felt restless and aimless. And more importantly, he didn't think it was honoring God. When asked what his next steps would be in an interview with *Relevant* magazine, he said, "Work with kids who have been rescued out of the slave trade . . . to go to a place where I'm a little bit more obscure, unknown—and just serve and care for some widows, orphans, and . . . really seek the Lord, really be alone with Him."[2]

What a minute, he wanted to leave the place where he was known, respected, and admired and go to a place where no one knew him? To serve those who had no way to reciprocate? Yes, this is exactly what he chose to do, and I think it creates a picture not only of the void we find in temporary prosperity, but the life we find when we truly follow Christ.

Like many people who achieve earthly fame and esteem, Francis Chan realized it did not fill the yearning in his soul. He knew receiving more of God meant more denial of anything that felt self-seeking or self-serving, and was willing to follow God into the unknown. He was ready to listen, even if it meant leaving something he spent years building.

The result was that he later went on to influence an even broader spectrum of people, write more books, and minister to others in ways he may have never thought possible. Going with God into unexplored territory was not the end, but the beginning.

> God exalts us when he looks at our hearts and sees someone who wants to encounter God rather than simply be noticed by people.

As I read about his story, I realized we don't have the power to exalt ourselves. The only true exaltation we can experience comes from God, and he gives it when he knows we are ready for it. God exalts us when he looks at our hearts and sees someone who wants to encounter God rather than simply be noticed by people. Then, he gives us a view unlike anything we've ever experienced. One that surpasses our wildest dreams. The way we acquire this view is not by furthering our own interests or advancing ourselves, but by embracing his plan for our lives. It's by submitting to his will, even when it doesn't make sense at the time. "Humble yourselves, therefore, under God's mighty hand, that he may lift you up in due time" (1 Pet. 5:6).

What a Humble Heart Looks Like

True humility can't be faked. Sure, we may be able to fool others for a time and perhaps even fool ourselves, but God always sees what our true intentions are. So what does a humble heart look like? And how do we maintain this attitude when God takes us on a journey that looks nothing like what we had planned for our lives? These are questions I spent many years of my life seeking the answers to.

For a long, painful season before starting a family, I had difficulty trusting God because I held onto past hurt and harbored bitterness over other questions. Questions that remained unanswered. Questions that I thought I needed solutions before I could move on. I'd grown up in a family where dysfunction was often prevalent as a result of drug addiction and codependency, and I longed for normalcy. I ached for God to seize my brother's life and get his attention in a such a transformative way that he would never want to turn to drugs again. And when this change didn't happen, I became angry. I wasn't sure exactly what a normal family looked like, but I was certain it was anything other than mine. For several years, I even turned to my own methods of self-medicating and convinced myself I could numb the pain with someone or something rather than releasing it to God. But no matter how hard I tried or how far I thought I'd removed myself from him, he was always there. And so was the pain.

After Chris and I moved cross-country and we had our first child, God gave me clarity. It wasn't all at once in a lightning bolt moment, but a steady opening of my eyes over my son's first year of life. But there was a step I had to take first. There was a decision I had to make. I had to surrender what I didn't understand to God. The part of me that wanted answers had to become less than the empty place in me that was hungry for God.

During the weeks following Jaden's birth, I was painfully aware of how this newborn was completely dependent on me. It was both terrifying and humbling. I was his source of food, his lullaby in the middle of the night, his warmth when he was cold. Slowly, I realized this baby boy was a representation of how God wanted me to be in my relationship with him. Completely dependent for my life, my breath, and my joy. Made whole not because I had all the remedies to life's questions, but because of my faith.

> If we want to see God clearly, our thirst for him must become greater than our thirst for answers.

If we want to see God clearly, our thirst for him must become greater than our thirst for answers. Few women understood this truth more than Saint Therese of Liseaux, who lived in the late nineteenth century and died of tuberculosis at the young age of twenty-four. Although her life was short, she is one of the most revered saints of all time, as a life-transforming encounter with God at fourteen caused her to devote all of her years to serving him and making his love known. She became known as "Little Flower" because her identity was rooted in Christ and she saw herself as one of his many unique creations. Although her disease rendered her body weak and prevented her from being able to do many tasks, her intimacy with God and complete dependence on him became the characteristic that drew others to him.

One of her most famous quotes is reflective of the realization that love for God matters more than works: "What matters in life is not great deeds, but great love."

Like Saint Therese, I had to let go of my need for understanding the whys of God's plan. As a young girl who'd been diagnosed with an illness that was incurable at the time, Saint Therese could've demanded answers or become bitter. She could have let her lot in life push her away from God's love instead of drawing her into it. But she chose love, and because of her choice, people are still talking about her heroism today.

Once I released my own hurt to God and trusted his will more than my need for understanding, I saw that true humility comes with three key realizations.

1. God's Knowledge Exceeds Our Own

Pride tells us we have to understand everything. It tells us we need answers, and if God doesn't give them, he's callous and uncaring. But here's the truth, even though it may be tough to swallow: God doesn't owe us an explanation. He's given us life, himself, and freedom, but he never promised that following him would mean a trouble-free existence here on earth. He demonstrated this truth when Job, who lost everything he had and was dealing with practically unbearable physical agony, demanded a reason from the Lord.

> If I have sinned, what have I done to you,
>> you who see everything we do?
> Why have you made me your target?
>> Have I become a burden to you? (Job 7:20)

Eventually, after chapters of Job's questions and pleas, God responds. And his reply might seem heartless, but I believe he is not speaking to Job out of a lack of concern, but a desire to show Job how little he comprehends what takes place in the heavenly world.

> Where were you when I laid the earth's foundation?
>> Tell me, if you understand.
> Who marked off its dimensions? Surely you know!
>> Who stretched a measuring line across it? (Job 38:4–5)

When Job responds, he says, "Surely I spoke of things I did not understand, things too wonderful for me to know" (Job 42:3). A divine encounter with the Lord brings recognition not only of his own conceit, but also of God's sovereignty. He sees that he doesn't have to understand everything about God and his reasons to worship him. It is enough to acknowledge who God is.

2. God Is Good, Even When Life Is Messy

We live in a world where our enemy still has power. He spends his days deceiving anyone who is willing to follow his schemes, and he takes his time pinpointing what our weaknesses are. But his days are limited. His reign on this planet will not last forever, and one day Jesus will return to claim those who are his. He will restore what was lost. Many times, we confuse evil in this world for a lack of power or concern from God. We forget he has given humans the ability to make their own choices, and they can choose to love him or ignore him.

Whether we realize it or not, we often use the messiness and chaos of life as an excuse to level the playing field between ourselves and God. We think since things are a mess anyway and it doesn't appear as though God is doing anything about it, we don't need him. We try to fix our situation on our own or stop coming to him in prayer. However, life's troubles are intended to have the exact opposite effect on us. God uses them to show us our need for him. To bring us to him in honest conversation and dependence on his Word that brings hope.

> When we allow life's messes to humble us instead of distance us, we come closer to the heart of God.

When we allow life's messes to humble us instead of distance us, we come closer to the heart of God. It's then that we realize it's impossible for him to do anything other than love us. He *is* love. He does not create chaos, but brings order and discernment. He gives us what we need as we recognize him as the source of all wisdom, discernment, and guidance. Humbling ourselves before our Maker is not intended to humiliate, but to make us the truest version of ourselves.

3. Our Power Comes from the Spirit, Not Ourselves

Whenever my kids have a question they're unable to answer on their own, they come to me or Chris. To them, we are an endless source of knowledge. Although my oldest son is slowly learning we don't know everything, he hasn't yet reached the age where we don't know anything. That phase will come later, and he can delay for as long as he likes.

When I think of my kids' thirst for information and dependence on us for it, it is a beautiful representation of what our relationship with the Spirit should look like. If we've received Christ, he is in us. An endless supply of power, wisdom, and counsel. And yet we often don't even acknowledge he's there. We go about our days as though we have to make every decision, face every trial, and encounter every stressful circumstance on our own. Why? Why do we live as though we're orphans, when we have a Helper who is always there?

Although I think there are many different reasons, one of the common ones is pride. Pride tells us we don't need help. It tells us we're capable of doing it all on our own, even when our lives are falling apart all around us. This distorted way of thinking can cripple us and make us carry burdens we were never intended to bear. But you know what? God invites us to lay it all down. Asking for help is not a sign of weakness, but one of strength, and freedom follows this key realization.

Even Jesus asked for help during his final hours here on earth. He experienced more emotional distress than you or I can imagine, and he knew he was vulnerable. "'My soul is overwhelmed with sorrow to the point of death,' he said to them. 'Stay here and keep watch'" (Mark 14:34). Even though the disciples didn't fulfill Jesus's request because they kept falling asleep, I think the fact that Jesus asked them for support shows the significant need for this type of humility in our own lives.

Jesus also asks for help from another source: his Father. He pleads for the cup to be taken from him, and we know the end of the story. The bitter cup remained. But even though the Father didn't give Jesus the help he wanted, he did give him the help he needed. How do I know? Because he completed the task he was sent to earth to do. Because he had the power of the Holy Spirit within him, and when he went to the Father in earnest prayer, that power was activated to an even greater degree.

Despite wanting another way, Jesus ends his prayer with an expression of obedience. And this is what sets him on a course of victory. This is what keeps him from picking up his divinity as he hangs on a cross and people hurl insults at him, question his identity, and mock him. He was a servant to the Father and a servant to us, filled with perfect love that stretched from before creation to all of eternity.

> Humbling ourselves before the Father exalts
> the power of the Holy Spirit within us.

This same power that kept Jesus focused is in us too. But we have to ask for it. We have to realize our need for it. Humbling ourselves before the Father exalts the power of the Holy Spirit within us. And we have to see it's set in motion not by demanding our own will, but submitting to his.

The Highest Place

Jesus's story didn't end on the cross. Because of his obedience, the Father gave him all authority in heaven and on earth; and one day, he will return with a different title than the one he came with the first time: King.

Therefore God exalted him to the highest place
    and gave him the name that is above every name,
that at the name of Jesus every knee should bow,
    in heaven and on earth and under the earth,
and every tongue acknowledge that Jesus Christ is Lord,
    to the glory of God the Father. (Phil. 2:9–11)

When you and I submit to God's will, our story keeps getting better too. Sometimes he exalts us and gives us a little glimpse of heaven. But like all things holy and sacred, a glimpse is all we can handle for now. Remember Paul and the thorn in his flesh? He saw unspeakable things and witnessed a heavenly splendor most people only dream about. God didn't humble him out of indignant anger or piety. He humbled him because it was through his weakness that his power and glory would shine the most. He knew Paul would not gain any followers through boasting of his own ability, but by reminding him of his humanness.

If God chooses to raise us up and reveal more of himself, it is never about receiving accolades or bragging rights. It's so others can see him through us. God elevates our perspective so that through our vision, others may be exalted too. Our experience becomes a bridge for others to cross over and witness the miraculous. And as we watch them transform, our view of him becomes clearer too. We see the unlimited vastness of his power and his ability to use what we thought was our own. Then, he humbles us once more. But this time, instead of grumbling, we thank him for it.

Adjusting Our Lens

1. Is there a situation or painful set of circumstances you are holding on to? Are you unable to forgive someone in your

life who caused you pain? Talk to God about it. He is ready to listen.

2. Can you think of a specific time in your life when humbling yourself and serving others gave you a better view of God? What did it look like? How did the way you viewed God change as a result of the experience?

12

We Have Everything Because of Him

I once heard one of my favorite authors say he still has night-mares where no one shows up to his book signings.[1] This man has written many *New York Times* best sellers. He's been on *The Today Show*, has a thriving ministry, travels the world, and nearly every book he writes sells hundreds of thousands of copies. You may have heard of him. His name is Max Lucado.

When I heard Max say this, part of me was relieved. I appreci-ated his transparency, and found comfort knowing I wasn't alone in this battle with doubt. At the time, writing was still new for me and I was experiencing a lot of self-defeating thoughts and frus-tration with the time it took to grow an audience. The fact that a well-seasoned, successful writer went through the same struggles reassured me that it was common and gave me much-needed fuel for the journey. But another part of me wondered, "Do we ever reach a place of success where doubt isn't an issue?"

Here was a person most people would say had reached the pinnacle of his career. He had more accolades than most writers achieve in a lifetime. He was releasing one book per year with a major publisher, with each one hitting the top of the charts. And yet uncertainty about the future still woke him in the middle of the night. Fear of walking into an empty room with no support gripped him when his mind drifted off to sleep. Could any relief be found for the journey? Was there ever an end to the endless uncertainties?

In short, no. This is a truth I've learned again and again over the years. But there's a major difference between this author and a myriad of others who deal with doubt and fear: he knew the truth. He had a weapon. When his flesh was tempted to succumb to weakness and lies, his spirit clung to the Rock that declared freedom.

You see, Max realized something many people spend a lifetime not knowing. There will always be another level of success. Another rung on the ladder. Another accolade to receive. We can keep reaching with both hands, trying to get to the top, only to find there is no summit. It's an endless race, and it will never satisfy the yearning for validation we all crave.

God knows we have this ache. After all, we are created in his image and he knew us before the creation of the earth. Wanting to achieve success is not the problem. The problem comes when we expect it to fill the hidden places in our souls that can only be satisfied by him.

When we base our value on the praise of others, it's difficult to see our value in Christ. A lack of affirmation may make us wonder if we'd misheard him when we took on that project or started that ministry. But Scripture doesn't say the value of our lives is found in others. It never tells us our lives are displays to be critiqued by others who will affirm whether what we're doing has merit. In today's world of Instagram memes, tweets, and Snapchat streaks, this is difficult to grasp because we are a culture hungry for an audience. However, Scripture tells us we died. Once we received Christ as our Savior, we died and our lives are now "hidden with Christ" (Col. 3:3). Our security isn't found in what others do or don't say, but in the Spirit.

> When we base our value on the praise of others, it's difficult to see our value in Christ.

So can we be sure we're fulfilling God's will, even when others don't applaud for us when we take a step of faith? How can we know he's near when everything in us cries out for approval? If we want to not only perceive God's presence but also find peace and rest, we must recognize where our works begin. Because they don't begin where we might think.

Our Works or His?

When we read a passage enough times, we may think we know it. We may even believe there's nothing left for us to learn about it. Since I spent my middle and high school years at a Christian school where Scripture memorization and study were required, I'm sad to say I've made this assumption on more than one occasion. But over the past several years, God has shown me that his Word is, in fact, living. His Spirit brings it to life. He brings fresh vision and knowledge from the words, often while reading verses I've known for years.

This happened to me a few weeks ago when I was reading in Ephesians and came to a Scripture I've read many times: "For we are God's masterpiece. He has created us anew in Christ Jesus, so we can do the good things he planned for us long ago" (Eph. 2:10 NLT). Most of the time when I had studied this verse in the past, the emphasis was on the word "masterpiece." Many speakers and authors I'd heard address this Scripture also highlighted how the original Greek word used in the place of "masterpiece" was "poiema," which can be translated to our English word "poem."[2] Every bit of this information was fascinating to me. I am a poem? I love poems! How cool is that? Can you hear the inner voice chiming, "I am so great. Me, me, me"?

While it's important to recognize our significance and the great love God has for us, there's another facet to this verse, which is equally important. In all of the reading and studying I did on these words, somehow one simple detail always escaped my notice: the works that were making me into this grand masterpiece or poem were not mine. They weren't a result of some grand plan I'd devised or a brilliant idea I'd conceived and brought to God saying, "Here, God. Bless this." Although, I have to admit, I've done this. And being the gracious, merciful God he is, he answered these prayers a few times. But despite my taking ownership, the plans were God's all along. He saw them before I was a promise of new life in my mother's womb. They were his vision, being enacted and carried out by me. My job was to listen. To be willing, even when the accolades and acknowledgments didn't come.

As we begin to see these plans as God's instead of our own, a shift takes place. Our perspective goes from being focused on self—our successes and our failures—to being focused on God and his invitation. He invites us to be part of what he's done. We see we are his instruments, being used to do amazing things and to point others toward his unchanging love and character. Recognition may come or it may not; but when it does, we turn it back to him. We give him the thanks. Because it was his to begin with.

If we think the works we do each day are our own, we . . .

- Worry about others' opinions, thinking they need to affirm us
- Try to predict outcomes we can't control
- Doubt ourselves and are always seeking the next nod of approval

But if the works we're doing each day are God's design, we can . . .

- Hold onto accolades lightly, realizing they belong to him
- Realize some failures are part of his plan too, because they grow us and teach us to rely solely on him
- Transform self-doubt into praise, because we get to participate in something eternal and infinitely bigger than ourselves

By realigning our thinking about whose plans we're carrying out, our entire attitude can change. Our focus goes from being centered on our own failures and successes to being centered on the next step God has for us. No, it won't happen overnight. There will still be days when we feel discouraged because we don't see the fruit we thought would result from our efforts. But when those days come, we can pick ourselves back up. We can press forward, because we know we've done what God asked us to do. We can rest secure in our position with him, which doesn't change with the highs and lows of this world.

Our Position in Him

When we're doing God's work instead of our own, our position doesn't change. It is fixed. Sealed by his Spirit. But to be honest, I haven't always lived like someone secure in my position with Christ. For a long chapter of my life, I lived like someone struggling to attain it. As if he would take away my security in him at any time if I didn't measure up to an invisible standard I created in my mind. Somewhere between having our second son and making a commitment to write full time, I became like the little girl walking out of my high school principal's office all over again. Tired. Defeated. Full of uncertainty.

But the more I walk this road of following Jesus, the more I see that he relentlessly pursues us. If we're living under the weight of lies keeping us from a life of freedom, he fights to bring us back to the truth. He fights for what's his, and leaves the ninety-nine in search of one sheep who's meandering through the darkness (Matt. 18:12). This is exactly what he did for me several years ago when I was going through a season of stress, unrealistic expectations, and disappointment.

We were expecting our third child, who was a surprise gift. At twenty weeks, we learned our third was a girl. We were raising two boys at the time, and my eyes teared up at the sonogram tech's words.

Aside from preparing for a baby, I was working on a huge writing project. My goal was to finish it before going into labor, and I worked until the point of exhaustion many evenings, trying to finish on time. I was also involved with both the women's ministry and children's ministry at our church, along with various after-school activities. In the months leading up to our daughter's birth, I felt God repeatedly tell me, "Slow down." It wasn't an audible voice, but a firm nudge in my spirit. Still, I continued full throttle, not wanting to let anyone down. The thought of disappointing anyone who was depending on me gave me anxiety. After all, if I didn't do all these things, who would?

I was striving for validation and recognition. Whether it came from people in the church, other writers, or friends, I longed to be seen. For people to pat me on the back and say, "Well done." And while I truly thought I was serving the Lord and showing my love for him, eventually I had to ask myself, "Does a person who's serving Jesus out of love constantly feel insecure, tired, and worn out? Does she feel resentful at what's on her plate?"

The answer was obvious, and something had to change. So, in the weeks leading up to the birth of our baby girl, I slowly began removing things. I stepped away from the MOPS leadership team at our church for a season. The writing project was shelved for a few months, and I focused on the huge transition our family faced. Instead of spending time worrying about disappointing others or filling my need to be needed, I stayed where I was needed the most.

Elise Skylar made her appearance the day after Thanksgiving via a scheduled C-section. As much as I wanted a natural delivery, things didn't work out as planned. Surgery meant more time was required to heal. It meant slowing down even more than I had initially intended, and recognizing God's plan was better than my own.

As we entered the Christmas season, our family spent a lot of time at home. It was quiet. It was peaceful. But it was also incredibly lonely at times, and there were days the doer in me twitched from lack of activity, even though I knew what I needed was rest.

One night when Elise was up several times, I sat in the glider, rocking her and humming a lullaby while she drifted off to sleep. My entire body felt heavy from exhaustion, and though my bed beckoned, I lingered there, marveling at her tiny features, her perfect purse-like lips, and her gurgling noises. And I realized something. She didn't have to do anything for me to love her other than exist.

As I savored the sweetness of the daughter I'd prayed for, I felt a gentle but clear nudge in my spirit saying, "You don't have to do anything for me to love you either. Just be. Let me love you." I was so tired from striving to be seen, I could have wept.

> In all of our striving to make ourselves visible
> to others, we are never invisible to God.

In all of our striving to make ourselves visible to others, we are never invisible to God. He sees us and cares for us, even when we don't see him. And the love I felt for my daughter that night was only an inkling of the love he feels for me. The love he feels for each of us. Not because of anything we've done, but because of who he is. This type of love changes us from the inside out, because instead of living our lives to be recognized, we live our lives as an expression of our confidence as his beloved.

Come and Sit

In Scripture, we often find Jesus dining with others. Whether the table is filled with sinners, his disciples, or friends, a meal with Jesus is a common Gospel scene where he often tells stories and parables. It's a place of intimacy and fellowship, where those who didn't know him had the opportunity to meet with him face to face. Can you imagine sitting with him now? What do you think he would say to you? While you and I don't have the ability to dine with Christ in a literal sense, we do have a seat as his table. Once we've made him Lord of our lives, we're guaranteed a place with him, and there's no amount of works or lack of works that can take it away.

> And God raised us up with Christ and seated us with
> him in the heavenly realms in Christ Jesus, in order that
> in the coming ages he might show the incomparable
> riches of his grace, expressed in his kindness to us in
> Christ Jesus. (Eph. 2:6–7)

In her book *Seated with Christ*, Heather Holleman explains the significance of these words, noting the verb "seated" is in the past tense. In other words, it's already been done. It's not something that's going to take place as a result of works we will or won't do. It's finished. Complete.

> We've already been seated in the heavenly realms, yet
> here we remain in the physical body in a material world.
> Paul often put theological truths in the past tense to
> affirm the certainty of them happening at a future date,
> and he maintained the same simultaneity that I feel
> when I read this verb. It's a both now-and-not-yet kind
> of verb.[3]

Even though we will not physically enter into the kingdom of God until we leave this life, we are already a part of it. Our place there exists not just in the future tense, but also in the present. We can live in full enjoyment and expectation of our place at his table, knowing it is fixed and secure. It's not going anywhere.

I don't know about you, but there are times when instead of living as though I'm affirmed by God, I live as though I have something to prove. What if we stopped fighting for what is already ours and took our seat? What would that look like?

I believe that when women grab hold of the truth that we don't have to fight to prove we have all we need, we will exercise freedom. Because of his Son's finished work, not because of anything we've done or can do, we have it all. When others don't give us the recognition we crave, we can rest in our position with Jesus. When we don't get the promotion we think we deserve at work, we can know without a doubt that God sees our efforts.

> Until we understand that only Christ can give
> us the validation we crave, we will constantly
> run in circles looking for others to fill us.

Until we understand that only Christ can give us the validation we crave, we will constantly run in circles looking for others to fill us. Our eyes must shift from our perceived worth to his view of us. Why? Because the validation others give us is fleeting. It is here one day and gone the next. Christ, on the other hand, gives us a position that is eternal. The world can't take it away because the world didn't give it to us.

What would living out this truth in our everyday lives look like? If we focused on our permanent position in Christ instead of our temporary position here on earth, how would our days be different? To answer this question, I had to claim this truth about my identity for myself. And I was surprised by how radically different my attitude became.

Living as a Daughter

If we're going to live as though we're sons and daughters of God, we have to completely transform our thinking. We live in a world where we're constantly told we have to measure ourselves. Whether it's against our sister or a celebrity who works with a personal trainer five days a week, the message is always there. Compare. Be like this person. Get more. Do more. Be more.

But Jesus simply says, "Come. Come as you are. You have everything because of what I did on the cross." As a result, we *can* be more because his Spirit lives in us, not because of some invisible measuring stick.

While this is the absolute best news ever, this truth isn't going to get into our minds by osmosis or by wanting to believe it. As

Paul says, we must be transformed. And transformation isn't something that happens on its own. It means meditating on the good and removing the bad.

> Do not conform to the pattern of this world, but be
> transformed by the renewing of your mind. Then you
> will be able to test and approve what God's will is—his
> good, pleasing and perfect will. (Rom. 12:2)

Do you notice promise here? By renewing our minds, we not only get to walk in freedom, but we can know what God's will is. We don't have to question it or buckle under the weight of others' misunderstanding. We can be confident. We can walk in his light, knowing he has our backs.

But how do we transform our minds? When we're bombarded with lies and half-truths in every direction we look, how do we cling to what's real? We begin by immersing ourselves in the source of truth: his Word. Since I struggled with my identity, I clung to verses about who I was in Christ.

This meant when I woke up, I reminded myself who I was. When I came face-to-face with a person or a situation where I questioned who I was, I repeated his Word in my mind. Sometimes, when the lies and contradictions were many, I took it a step further and spoke it out loud.

Speaking God's Word out loud is a powerful weapon. It not only does wonders to dispel the darkness threatening to overtake our minds, but it also reinforces what's excellent, praiseworthy, and lovely and secures our feet onto his solid ground. Jesus himself said, "For the mouth speaks what the heart is full of" (Matt. 12:34). The opposite is also true. When we speak truth, it gets into our hearts and minds. Instead of living like a person who is fragmented, working as though our mind, body, and soul are three separate persons, the straightforward task of uttering his Word out of our mouths enables us to do what he commanded us to do: love him with all our heart, soul, and mind. It helps us to live as one complete being.

> If you want to transform life that's been polluted by lies, speaking God's truth is an irrefutable remedy.

If you want to transform life that's been polluted by lies, speaking God's truth is an irrefutable remedy. When I spoke God's truth, I was able to contrast it to the lies we often hear about ourselves:

Truth	Lie
I am holy and blameless before God. (Eph. 1:4)	I must work to prove myself.
I am a child of God and coheir with Christ. (Rom. 8:17)	I am an orphan.
He leads me to triumph and knowledge of him. (2 Cor. 2:14)	My success is solely up to me.
In Christ, I am free from the yoke of slavery. (Gal. 5:1)	I am a slave to my highs and lows.

While living out these truths is a continual battle, it starts with claiming them. It begins with speaking them out loud in our everyday lives not only when things are difficult and we're struggling to remember, but when we're high on the tails of a victory.

My prayer is that, eventually, his Word will become as much a part of who we are as breathing. It will become like the air in our lungs, giving us life the same way he breathed into us when he created us from the dust. Then we can cheer for our sister's victory when she gets her dream job without sulking because we're still waiting for a promotion. We can walk with our heads held high, even when our boss doesn't acknowledge the extra time we put into that project.

We can do this not only because we're one body, but also because we have everything. Security. Immovable position. Endless love. A seat at the table with the King of Kings. And when we know what we have, we can let go of what we think we're missing. It fades like a dream you can't remember the moment you open your eyes. As much as you try to grasp it, it's fuzzy and the details are blurred. Then suddenly, you don't need to recall it anymore. Because you realize your own life is right in front of you, and it's better than a dream.

Adjusting Our Lens

1. If you look back on your life, can you identify a moment when there was one position or success you craved that you thought would satisfy a yearning in your soul? If you achieved it, how did it make you feel? Was the feeling temporary or permanent?

2. Practice telling yourself who you are in Christ when you wake up each morning and whenever you feel like you have to measure yourself against someone else. Use some of the truths outlined in this chapter, or other favorite verses about our identity. Then, record how they change your attitude. Did they help you refocus?

13

The One Sure Way They'll See Jesus

I stared at the text message on my phone, not sure how to respond. My friend was avoiding me, and I didn't know why. My mind ran through the last dozen interactions we had like a Rolodex, wondering if I somehow offended her.

When was the last time we had a conversation that didn't seem forced or tense? When was the last time we went to lunch or a playdate?

I couldn't remember. My lack of control over the whole situation made me uncomfortable. But I knew aside from confronting her, there was little else I could do. I prayed for God's wisdom and discernment, taking deep breaths to avoid tears. I also prayed that if there was something I'd done to cause a rift between us, I wouldn't let pride keep me from taking responsibility for my actions.

Weeks went by and I buried myself in a writing project, trying to keep my mind off the topic. When I saw my friend at MOPS and church, I attempted to get a reading on her heart, but was left in the dark. Our relationship remained cordial but there was a noticeable barrier between us. While most others probably didn't notice, it was obvious to me. I missed the bond and the close friendship we once shared. I knew if things didn't change at some point, I would need to approach her with my concern.

The more time I spend on this earth, the more I realize something: relationships matter to God. Jesus's earthly ministry was spent cultivating relationships with his followers, with those around him, and with his Father. But often, we don't see the fruit of our time, efforts, and emotional investment. Despite the love and energy we pour into our friends and neighbors, we may not always know whether we're making a difference in their lives.

The note or gift we sent in the mail may arrive without a response. The offer to help with the kids or help with the move to a new house may be declined. This doesn't mean our efforts weren't noticed, and there are endless reasons why people respond or don't respond in a certain way. But sometimes we still mull over the situation and worry. All the unknowns and the whys can make us a little crazy.

Kids are a perfect example of this. I can't tell you the number of times I've explained something to one of my boys and received blank stares in return. Or the number of times I've tried to soothe my daughter from a restless night of teething only to be met with screams and a hand that fights my attempts to comfort. Do these reactions mean my efforts don't matter? Of course not. And the same is true for yours. But they can definitely discourage our weary souls and make us question our abilities and our "want" to invest in the relationships we cultivate in our family and other circles.

We may wonder how we're qualified to parent, minister, or make a difference in the context of the relationships we find ourselves in. We may think we're not the right person to share the love of Christ with the new mom in our moms group or to initiate a Bible study or life group at church. And trust me, the enemy loves nothing more than to use our discouragement as an opportunity to derail what only God can bring about in these intimate relationships in these settings.

So how do we know others see Jesus? How can we be confident he's reaching others through us, even when we're left staring at our phones, waiting for a response from a friend? We can know because he speaks to us.

In John 10:27 Jesus says, "My sheep listen to my voice; I know them, and they follow me."

> Our confidence in our ability to hear God's voice must become greater than the voice of doubt.

Although it says it right here in black and white, we sometimes question this truth, don't we? We ask ourselves, "Was God really asking me to do that? Or was it just me? Was it just in my head?" Our confidence in our ability to hear God's voice must become greater than the voice of doubt. I can't tell you the number of times he's asked me to do something, but when I didn't receive affirmation or encouragement from others, I second-guessed it was from him. There's also another voice that often distracts us: the voice of the deceiver. Sometimes it's difficult to know which voice is true.

Although I'm still a work in progress and I stumble every day, God has shown me a few ways to know something was from him, even when others don't respond the way I want or anticipate.

When we second-guess something was from him, we can ask ourselves these questions:

- Were you sure the nudge to act was from God before you saw others' reactions?
- Did what he was asking you to do line up with what he says in his Word?
- Was your motivation to love and point others to him or to receive praise?

Friend, wanting affirmation is human and God sees this need. He won't let it go unacknowledged. He knows we need encouragement to press on when we're not sure we're making a difference. But when the confirmation doesn't come, know this: it mattered. He made an impact through you watering the seeds he's planted through your life.

My friend Crystal volunteered as a helper in the two- and three-year-olds' class for months until one day she felt sure God was calling her to teach. She didn't have children of her own yet, but she loved kids and they loved her too. Whenever I walked by the classroom, she always had a smile on her face, no matter how crazy and hyper the kids were. One day, I stepped in to help her for a few minutes while one of the workers went to the bathroom. I was moved by the grace and patience she exhibited toward the class, even when she had to repeat instructions. She's one of the few women in the children's ministry who does not serve out of a sense of obligation, but because she truly enjoys being around young people.

Several months ago, Crystal shared with me how she didn't feel qualified to teach children and wondered whether anything she was teaching the kids was sinking in. Children's ministry can be a pretty thankless job, and often the volunteers feel discouraged. Morale can get low quickly. Despite the uncertainty she felt, she continued teaching. She knew the pastor's wife, who normally led the class, needed time away to recharge and listen to the service.

One day, out of the blue, a mom with a boy in the class thanked her. She told Crystal how every night for the past few weeks her son prayed. He prayed for Crystal, his friends, and his family. He had never done this before coming to Crystal's class. It was huge. He was practicing exactly what he'd been learning with the other kids; but until this parent said something, Crystal had no idea. She didn't realize the way her simple act of following a nudge from God was changing hearts and lives.

Tears formed in her eyes as she told me about the conversation with this boy's mom. My eyes teared up too. Jesus was moving and guiding young hearts, even in the midst of her doubt. While Crystal questioned if anything she was teaching the kids was getting into their heads, he was working. And he brought the evidence of it in his time, when she needed it most.

Don't Dilute Perfection

There's an old Sunday school story I heard years ago. A teacher was asking her students to name a creature and she gave them various clues. "This animal makes its home in trees and has a long, bushy tail. It likes to bury nuts and can be found in urban areas. His face is similar to a chipmunk, but it's usually larger and does not burrow holes into the ground."

"Do you know what it is?" the teacher asks. She looks around the classroom in anticipation. There's a lesson she wanted to share. A kid's hand shot up. He knew the answer. Or, so he thinks. With seeming frustration he says, "Well, it sounds like a squirrel but this is Sunday school, so it must be Jesus!"

Now, this scenario usually cues some chuckles, but how similar are we? Only in our case, the answer to how others will see Jesus *is* Jesus. They see him as we live our lives motivated by our love for him instead of our need for acknowledgment. But we try to come up with a different answer. We know the gospel. We know the greatest commandments are to love God and love others. But we complicate it. We dilute it. When we don't receive the appreciation we desire, we become frustrated. Whether it's a spouse who doesn't show gratitude for our work around the house or a child who doesn't respond to discipline, there are endless ways life can make us lose sight of our purpose. Our culture teaches us to love only when it's reciprocated, but others see Jesus in us when it's without reserve.

> Our culture teaches us to love only when it's reciprocated, but others see Jesus in us when it's without reserve.

A few years ago, while volunteering in a couple of local and online ministries, I became extremely discouraged. The moms group I helped lead received complaints from its attendees on a regular basis. Some of them were as simple as not liking the craft we completed that day while others were more serious and difficult to navigate. While sorting through the issues, I also dealt with problems in an online writing group I led. The weekly critiques lacked participation, causing those who regularly contributed to become frustrated. I questioned whether I should continue helping in these various ministries or simply focus on my family.

I knew my family was a ministry in and of itself and was worth the bulk of my time and energy, but even within the confines of my own home, I seemed to hit a wall. While we awaited the birth of my third child, my second son struggled to learn basic skills in school. I searched for ways to help him grasp the material, but his lack of focus and disinterest further exasperated me.

In these types of situations, my tendency is to navigate between two extremes. The first is to find the easiest way out. How do I solve the problem with the least amount of effort possible? How do I make the moms happy? What can I use to bribe my son and make him want to learn? The other is to simply avoid the issue. I bury my head and hope it will go away. But you know what? Here's the thing. Time and experience has shown me neither of these approaches works very well in the end. Although they may serve to temporarily blanket the issue and take my mind off it, trouble will eventually resurface. And often, it's worse than it was before.

I call these alternate approaches the appeasing and avoiding cycle. They operate like a treadmill, causing us to expend a lot of energy without ever taking us anywhere.

Appeasing:	Avoiding:
Make everyone happy, no matter what	Lots of nodding, smiling
Don't ask whether the complaint or need can be addressed by someone else	Does nothing to address issue
Use bribery if needed to get desired result	Waits for issue to resolve itself

But you know what? God showed me a better way. And it yields an abundantly better outcome.

Instead of starting with myself, I start with him. I start with his love. I start with Jesus. Now, I realize this may sound over-simplistic and trite, so let me explain. In all my anxiousness over the issues in ministry and at home, I wasn't looking to God. I was looking to myself. I was taking all the weight of responsibility on my shoulders, causing me to feel tense and lacking the ability to fix it.

My mind was a repeated circle of thoughts that sounded something like this:

No one appreciates that I'm volunteering my time for this ministry.

No one sees Jesus or the difference I'm trying to make.

I may as well quit. I'm not accomplishing anything that is worthwhile for him.

I'm not qualified to work in ministry.

One day, as I was studying the Word and writing, I felt a gentle nudge from God. It wasn't condemning or callous. But with a simple question, I immediately knew why I felt so defeated.

"Are you trying to make me look good or make yourself look good?"

I knew the answer. And I knew I needed to make a change.

When our love for God motivates us, everything else falls into place. When our desire for affirmation motivates us, we run in circles. While our feelings and the praise of others changes and fades, God's noticeable favor on us doesn't. Others will see him and his love for them as we continue to press forward on the course he has for us, regardless of setbacks and bumps in the road.

Jesus knew our tendency to let the details of our lives get out of order. He knew that when stress mounts, our tendency is to look to ourselves and try to take the weight of the situation on our shoulders. This is why he specifically addresses this issue in Matthew when he says, "But seek first his kingdom and his righteousness, and all these things will be given to you as well" (Matt. 6:33).

This principle applies whether we're talking about clothes, money, ministry problems, or raising kids. So in the moms and writing groups, I asked myself, "Am I loving these women well? Am I putting their needs above my need to look good?" If the answer was yes, I didn't need to worry about whether someone complained or not. Because in the end, I had done what God asked me to do. And with my son, I asked, "How does he love? What gives him joy?" The answer? Play. Games. Fun. If I made learning into a game and made it fun, his desire to learn would come. When I found the answer to this question, I discovered how to teach him in a way his five-year-old brain could grasp.

Friends, most days we won't see the work God is doing in someone through us. We may not see how much a note we sent to them meant or how much they appreciated our help with the kids. Although God sometimes allows us to see glimpses of what he's doing, we're often left wondering whether the seeds we planted are yielding any fruit. I believe one of the reasons he does this is to keep us humble. To keep us dependent on him, and to prevent us from being prideful. It is only through his Spirit working in us and through us that we can change our perspective in our relationships and homes. This is not a reason to be disheartened, but encouraged. We have a Helper. He goes with us. And he invites us to participate in the beautiful plan he's writing.

> Our focus must shift from changing
> results to his unchanging love.

The characteristic of his heart that will draw others to him is his love. It's who he is. It's why he came. Our focus must shift from changing results to his unchanging love. When we're focused on his love instead of the outcome, we can . . .

- Know his love is constant, even when people's attitudes are not
- Know what he asks us to do (love) doesn't change, even if others don't love us back in a tangible way

- Know that his Spirit is always working, even when others don't appear to be changed

Others will see Jesus when our love looks different than what they're used to seeing. When we put his directive to "go and tell" above our desire to know what he's doing.

This love must be our reason to continue reaching out, even when we're losing hope. But you know that? When we experience doubt, he often sends encouragement at just the right time. Sometimes, when we are feeling down, we can ask him for a sign. If we keep our eyes open and watch for his hand, he surprises us with the limitless ways he answers this simple prayer.

Living as His Love

Our evening MOPS meeting was over, and I was busying myself with cleaning up. I helped stack chairs and folded tables as women had last-minute conversations before picking up their kids. As much as I tried to occupy my hands, my mind kept going back to my friend. It had been a few months and the distance between us still stood like a gaping hole. I was nervous about approaching her, but I didn't know what else to do. I silently prayed my words would be gracious and unoffending.

As she was exiting the sanctuary, I asked her if we could chat for a minute. We exchanged a few awkward words and then I quietly said, "Things have seemed off between us over the past few months. Is there something I did to offend you?"

At first she tried to make light of the situation and laugh it off. But I gently persisted, explaining why I felt like there was an unsaid tension. Finally, through tears, she explained that she was going through a difficult season. There was a darkness hanging over her, and she couldn't seem to pinpoint a cause or solution. I nodded and offered my support, knowing this place of hopelessness. I thought back to the days following the birth of my first son and remembered how I often wondered whether I'd make it through the day. I told her about my own experience and encouraged her to seek counseling if she didn't think the situation was improving. Most of all, I silently committed to praying for her. I knew my prayers were one of the most effective tools I could offer her, and I was also aware that there was a battle we couldn't see taking place.

Over the next few weeks, I prayed for my friend every time she came to mind. I prayed she'd be able to see his light and that she wouldn't be afraid to seek help if she needed it. I prayed for God to open her eyes to the truth of who she was in Christ, and not succumb to the lies of the enemy.

Then one day in early spring, I didn't make it past my morning coffee before I wanted to crawl back into bed. It was raining again and a heavy fog hung over our mountaintop. It seemed as though I was wading through my own fog too, and I couldn't seem to focus on the next thing I had to do. My kids dragged their feet as they were getting ready for school, and I lost my temper. We barely made it to the bus stop on time. I felt lost in the pile of laundry that never seemed to shrink. I was quickly spiraling into a dark pit of negative thoughts and realized my need to move my feet to solid ground again.

I sent up a simple prayer: "God, help." Out of the blue, I received a text from my friend. Her words were short and to the point. She thanked me for my prayers and told me she was starting to see the light again. Tears formed in my eyes at the realization: I never told her I would pray for her. But she knew I would. Without even asking, she knew.

Even though it was just a text, it meant everything. Despite the tension in our friendship, the awkwardness and hurt feelings, she recognized his love in me. She had confidence in what I would do as a friend. And her confidence reignited a fire to keep bringing the needs of his people to him. It reignited my desire to keep caring for others and taking risks, even when it didn't seem like it mattered.

With a simple text, I saw that he is always working in others' hearts, even when we don't realize it. Even when we doubt and question why we continue to pursue relationships, he is moving. His Spirit isn't dormant. We are told, "If we are faithless, he remains faithful, for he cannot disown himself" (2 Tim. 2:13).

This is not an excuse to be faithless, but an encouragement that our times of unbelief don't change the character of God. He never fails to deliver. His love is not moody, but perfect. When we fail or become discouraged or lose hope, he doesn't leave or decide to take a break. He's there, waiting for us to recognize he was there all along.

On a cool spring morning, he showed me his faithfulness through a text. I realized with awe that my prayers for my friend ended up answering my own prayer as well. All I had to do was send up a one-word plea. He reminded me that we're his ambassadors here on earth, and he's making his appeal through us. Sometimes it's on a stage. Sometimes it's across the ocean in a foreign land. And other times, it's right in our backyard, at a church where a friend needs someone to speak up and take notice.

A Light Burning Brightly

We often recognize that the times when God has been working through us all along aren't actually earth-shattering. We don't have to be on a platform in front of hundreds of people or even in a room where others can see us. We simply have to wake up each morning and say, "God, let me be a light for you. Use me to point others to you."

This is the prayer I pray almost every morning when I wake up. And you know what? Many days, I don't know if others have seen

Jesus in me or not. The laundry continues to pile up and some-times I forget to sign the kids' homework folders. I need grace each and every minute of the day. But I continue to put one foot in front of the other, knowing God lives in me and will work through me.

Do you know that you have this same power? It isn't reserved for a select few or for those who are standing behind a pulpit. God doesn't play favorites. His power is for each and every one of us who know him. And you know what? It works best when we reach the end of ourselves and we're not sure we have much more go-power in us. Not because he likes to see us suffer, but because this is when we reach for him and ask him to take over. When we ask for more of him and that power living within, he hears us. He delivers. He longs to ignite a fire within each one of us that will point others to the truth of who he is.

I don't want my light to burn any less brightly because I don't get a pat on the back. I want his oil to be the fuel for my flame. This oil is the nourishment that sustains, because it comes from his Spirit. And his Spirit is limitless. What the world gives, it can take away. But what God gives? It is eternal. It goes beyond the confines of this planet and never runs out.

Keep believing he is able to accomplish the good work he started in you. He's not finished yet. Don't look to the right or to the left, but straight ahead as you shine for him. Your radiance is one of a kind. His plan and his purpose for you are as unique as the stars he placed in the sky.

Even when you don't see fruit, keep working and trust he's working as well. So when he appears, you will stand confident, knowing you have used everything he's given you.

Adjusting Our Lens

1. Has there ever been a time when you reached out to help someone or committed someone to prayer but weren't sure it made a difference? Thank God for the work you know he's doing, even if you don't see it yet.

2. When you serve others in your home, community, or ministry, what is your motivation? Be completely honest here. If it's something other than a love for God and a desire to make him known, talk to God about it. His faithfulness will not change as a result of your confession. And you'll be amazed how he can work in your heart.

3. Have you ever found yourself in the appeasing and avoiding cycle? Did the situation improve or become worse? Write down one way you could choose Jesus and his love in that situation. Maybe it's approaching a friend or family member about a difficult situation or a tension in your relationship instead of avoiding them. Whatever it is, commit to taking that step.

4. Do you truly believe Jesus is the answer to what you want? What you desire? This doesn't mean you can't desire other things in life, but is he your first love? Take time to confess anything that is coming before him. Write it down and then write Jesus's name over it. Then, make a commitment to put whatever that thing is in its proper place. If you need to remove it from your life completely, ask someone to hold you accountable to carry through with it.

Acknowledgments

Writing a book is not an individual effort. This project was actually birthed over five years ago and was the result of much prayer, encouragement from dear friends and family, hard work, and perseverance. To everyone who has given me a push to keep going when the road was long and weary, thank you.

To my husband, Chris—thank you for being my biggest fan. You always teased me that you wanted a "sugar mama" for a wife, and while I'm not sure this gig will get you your wish, I do know that I wouldn't be here without your support.

To my parents—your continual prayers have been felt, and I knew they were always there, even without my asking.

To my brother, Daniel—you encouraged me to write for the Lord years ago when I didn't see how it was even possible, and I have never forgotten your prophetic words. Thank you for seeing the future I could not see for myself.

To my agent, Blythe—you pushed me to become a better writer and to dig deeper when I didn't think I had it in me. You believed in me, which was the greatest gift of all. Thank you for going above and beyond for your clients.

To the entire BDA team—I never imagined I'd be given the gift of a new writing family after joining a literary agency, but that's exactly what you've become. I love the way each of us supports each other on this crazy adventure, and holds each other up in prayer when we need it most.

To my kids, Jaden, Gabe, and Elise—you inspire me in so many ways and teach me more about God and his love than anyone. Thank you for making me a mom and for showing me what the love of a parent looks like.

To Betsy, Kristi, Kristine, Lisa, Lyli, and Tiffany—our Zoom chats have become a lifeline for me. Thank you for always being a safe place to share my fears and frustrations, but most of all for not leaving me there. Thank you for being a place of trust and truth, and for praying circles around me when I needed them most.

To the entire Leafwood team—thank you for welcoming me and taking the chance on a new writer who had a hunger and thirst to write for the Lord. The opportunity to share a book with the world is the fruition of a childhood dream, and I don't take it for granted.

To Kelly Balarie—your leadership and willingness to blaze trails has inspired me for as long as I've known you. Thank you for praying me out of the pit I was in, for your generous heart, and for your courageous faith. You are a gift, my friend.

To Katie Reid—your encouragement, friendship, and willingness to think through ideas and share your knowledge has been such a gift to me. You are such a blessing to my life, and it's been a joy to share this journey with you.

To Jami Amerine, Christy Mobley, Karina Allen, and Angela Parlin—your friendship will always hold a special place in my heart. I will never forget our Voxer chats, the encouragement and support. Each of you is part of this journey, and I love you dearly.

To my New Day Church family—you gave my family a place to call home when we felt like we had no anchor. You felt like family as soon as we walked in the door, the answer to a prayer I'd been praying for over two years. Thank you for being the hands and feet of Christ.

To the entire community at COMPEL—this journey started because of the guidance and next steps I received from your training. I had no clue what to do next, and your podcasts, interviews, and tips gave me the tools I needed to get to this point. Thank you Lysa TerKeurst and team for your dedication to new and experienced writers.

To the team at Hope*Writers—you make your writers feel right at home, no matter what stage they're in. Thank you for creating such a warm, welcoming environment to grow and to learn even more about writing, marketing, and everything in between.

To all my readers who have encouraged me to keep pursuing this dream even on the days when I wanted to give up—you are the reason I kept going. Your readership kept me showing up at the keyboard, day in and day out.

Most of all, thank you to God. All of this, every word and syllable, is for you. You didn't give up on me, even when I tried to run. Thank you for being a God who relentlessly pursues us, even when we don't want to be pursued. You are my everything.

About the Author

Abby McDonald is wife to Chris and the mom of two energetic boys and one sweet girl. After moving around the country several times, her family settled in western Maryland, where they enjoy the small town life, mountains, and camping with friends. Abby is active in ministry at her church and writes regularly on her blog. Her words have been featured in numerous publications, podcasts, and websites, including Proverbs 31 Ministries, (in)Courage, iBelieve, and Crosswalk.

Abby is known for her transparency and cut-to-the-heart-of-the-matter style as she encourages her readers to let go of comparison and embrace their unique, God-given identity. She proclaims the truth that none of us are ever too far from God; he pursues each one of us with the heart of a Father chasing after his child.

Abby would love to connect with you online at www.Abby Mcdonald.org, and you will receive a free gift when you sign up for email updates. You can also join her on Instagram, @abbymcd7, and on Facebook at www.facebook.com/fearfullymademom.

Endnotes

Chapter Two: Looking Past Our Expectations

[1] Christy Mobley, "When the Wrong Direction Leads to the Right Destination," *Joying in the Journey* (blog), October 26, 2017, http://christymobley.com/2017/10/26/when-the-wrong-direction-leads-to-the-right-destination/.

[2] Kathryn Ross, "When Doubt Rears Its Shadow," comment #5, *Abby McDonald* (blog), March 10, 2014, http://abbymcdonald.org/2014/03/when-doubt-rears-its-shadow/.

Chapter Three: Faith That Moves Our Feet Forward

[1] Misty Raines, Facebook, https://www.facebook.com/groups/lovefromukraine/.

Chapter Four: The Treasure That Takes Us beyond This World

[1] Kent Dobson, *NIV First-Century Study Bible* (Grand Rapids: Zondervan, 2014), 827.

Chapter Five: Hope in God's Plan or Our Own?

[1] Lisa Appelo, "Dealing with Grief," Premier Christian Radio, September 3, 2018, https://www.premierchristianradio.com/Shows/Weekday/Woman-to-Woman/Interviews/Dealing-with-Grief2/.

Chapter Six: The Power of Perspective

[1] Betsy de Cruz, "Keeping God at the Center of Your Dream," *God-Sized Dreams* (blog), February 18, 2015, http://www.godsizeddreams.com/keeping-god-at-the-center-of-your-dream/.

Chapter Eleven: How We Gain the Clearest View of God

[1] "The Second Wettest Spot on Earth, Mount Wai'Ale'Ale on Kaua'i," *Kukui'ula, South Shore, Kaua'i,* January, 27, 2015, https://kukuiula.com/mount-waialeale/.

[2] "The Crazy Mission of Francis Chan," *Relevant Magazine*, February 24, 2011, https://relevantmagazine.com/god/church/features/24816-the-crazy-mission-of-francis-chan.

Chapter Twelve: We Have Everything Because of Him

[1] Max Lucado, "Conversation with Max Lucado," *COMPEL Training*, October 6, 2015.

[2] Jon Bloom, "You Are God's Workmanship," *Desiring God* (blog), May 11, 2015, https://www.desiringgod.org/articles/you-are-gods-workmanship.

[3] Heather Holleman, *Seated with Christ: Living Freely in a Culture of Comparison* (Chicago: Moody Publishers, 2015), 27.